Overcoming Lyme Disease

The Truth About Lyme Disease
And The Hidden Dangers Plaguing
Our Bodies

By Jennifer Heath

To your healing!
+ success!
xo Heath
Jennifer Heath

First Edition 2017

Printed in the United States of America

Published by:
Positive Healing Publishing
P.O. Box 182
Chelsea, MI 48118
www.OvercomingLymeDisease.com

Cover and Interior Design by: Rory Carruthers Marketing

Project Management and Book Launch by: Rory Carruthers Marketing

www.RoryCarruthers.com

For more information about Jennifer Heath or to book her for your next event, speaking engagement, podcast or media interview please visit:
www.OvercomingLymeDisease.com

Dedication

This book is dedicated to all of the heroes out there. Those who are still fighting for their lives and can't get properly diagnosed as having Lyme disease or Post-Sepsis Syndrome. For those with their diagnoses who still see no end in sight. For those who have been fortunate enough to find relief in alternative treatments and have been restored to health.

Then there are the other heroes, the handful of medical doctors, along with holistic doctors, who have taken a stand, and every day, risk the loss of their license to help their patients suffering in silence. These saints keep learning and growing in knowledge to help their patients fight this awful and deadly disease.

All of these heroes have fought through the hypocrisy of Western Medicine, CDC lies, ALDF smear campaigns, insurance companies, and Big Pharma that have tied the hands of caring doctors who would love to help those with Lyme disease, but are threatened not to treat, or they will lose their medical license!

Let's not forget the angels out there, those who are standing by their spouses, family members, and loved ones who are battling this unacknowledged disease.

Most importantly, let us not forget the worst victims of this crime—those who have lost their lives to this disease because they couldn't get a proper diagnosis.

Table of Contents

Foreword

With the purchase of this book, you have chosen to enter the realm of Lyme disease, the most rapidly growing, vector-borne disease in the country and perhaps the world. Found on all continents of the planet, with the exception of Antarctica (the minuscule nymphs can't survive the extreme colds), and especially in countries and states with four seasons.

It was first "discovered" in 1975 in the small Connecticut town of Lyme in a cluster of teens who had developed a crippling type of sudden-onset arthritis. Using a microscope, a scientist, Dr. Willie Burgdorferi, discovered the causative agent to be a spirochete, a fine, wispy, worm-like organism from the same family of organisms that causes syphilis. The organism, Borrelia burgdorferi, was named after its discoverer. Remember this name.

Lyme disease has become the "great masquerader," capable of causing a myriad of symptoms and diseases that destroy one's health and bring utter confusion to physicians and diagnosticians alike.

Is this a new disease? Hardly. A mummified corpse discovered in the Alps several years ago was found to harbor the actual DNA (the genetic code) of the borrelia organism itself. This goes back five thousand years! Recent research implies a human– spirochete connection that may be entwined in our history for millions of years.

Are you ill? Have you been labeled as a hypochondriac or given a diagnosis of autoimmune disease? Do you have lupus? Have you seen a litany of physicians with no answers to your health issues? Consider the "great masquerader" (Lyme disease), the other syphilis, as the cause.

Diagnosing a borrelial infection is not a simple matter of a blood test. The first roadblock will be your physician. Most are not "Lyme literate." They are not familiar with this infectious disease as the norm, or they are taught that it doesn't exist at all. The Infectious Disease Society of America (specialists in infectious disease after special training—whatever that means) says that there is no such diagnosis as chronic Lyme disease.[1] In their opinion, two weeks of antibiotics will cure this now pandemic. This is simply not true, as verified in patients with chronic symptoms and the use of a microscope in which the observer with patience will see the organisms with his/ her own eyes.

In our state of Nevada, local physicians have become accustomed to parroting, "We don't have Lyme disease in Nevada." This is most likely due to the etiquette observed by the ticks at our borders! The ticks just turn around, leaving our state "germ-free."

Even if you were fortunate enough to convince your physician to draw the appropriate labs for Lyme testing, the results will most likely be negative—but a FALSE negative, meaning you most likely have the disease, but the lab says no, even though you are in a wheelchair, have Multiple Sclerosis, ALS or Alzheimer's disease.

These FALSE negative results are due to a number of reasons. There are upwards of three hundred or more different strains of

---

[1] "Updated Guidelines on Diagnosis, Treatment of Lyme Disease." *IDSA: Updated Guidelines on Diagnosis, Treatment of Lyme Disease.* Web. <http://www.idsociety.org/updated_guidelines_on_diagnosis_treatment_of_lyme_disease/>

this borrelial organism, and most labs, even the specialty Lyme testing labs, can't detect the antibodies your immune system should generate to fight the disease. This must change with technology. More importantly, Lyme disease, especially chronic Lyme disease, is incredibly immunosuppressive, meaning it prevents your immune system from mounting an antibody response to attack the invaders. Even more insidious is the ability of these bugs to "hide" in your tissues, especially your brain, CNS (central nervous system), musculoskeletal system (tendons, muscles, joints, ligaments), and cardiac tissue. The hardest "critters" to treat are the spirochetes that invade your red and white blood cells, live within these cells, and then eventually kill them.

The special "L-forms," or cell wall deficient type, shed their cell walls and totally disguise themselves from our immune system's defenders (neutrophils, macrophages, eosinophils) that patrol our tissues, dedicated to eliminating pathogens that would cause us disease. If our immune system can't see potential enemies, how can it defend us?

I was fortunate in my early years of medicine to have had Dr. Lida Mattman, PhD, as a mentor. This Nobel Laureate taught me how to use a microscope, as well as the cause of Multiple Sclerosis, ALS (Lou Gehrig's disease), and other autoimmune-type diseases. Using a darkfield microscope, a blood sample from a patient with a suspected disease can be observed "live" without staining or fixing, and eventually see the spirochetes of borrelia exiting the lining of the red blood cells! There's your diagnosis! If you see it with your eyes, you have the disease—contrary to what your labs (or the doctor) tell you. Unfortunately, a majority of physicians have never heard of a darkfield microscope, let alone know how to use one. It may take days of observation before one can see the causative agent of borrelia.

To further complicate matters, one is not infected with one type of spirochete. There can be several different types of spirochetes present. Most of the chronically ill have what I call "multiple infectious disease syndrome" with many co-infections present that synergistically act to slowly destroy your health. Babesia is a form of malaria that lives inside your red blood cells and can cause anemia, fever, chills, etc., then kill your cell. Bartonella is a "Cat scratch fever" on steroids that can render you full of rage, anger, and depression, while also leaving strange skin lesions that look like stretch marks. Medicine knows little of this disease. Let us not forget all of the viruses we all possess such as CME, Epstein-Barr, herpes, etc. that work in conjunction to render you lifeless. All of these immune invaders compromise our defenses. Slowly you are dying, yet few in the profession of medicine can provide you with any life-saving answers.

What can one do? Well, most oral antibiotics don't work well anymore. Some IV types do help when used in conjunction with other modalities, such as ozone, colloidal silver, autogenous vaccines, and others. Many patients need to have all dental infections removed, such as root canals and cavitations, before they get better. Many will need to be de-wormed; yes, eliminating big critters such as parasites, as you would deworm a farm animal or your dog. Stop the bugs feasting on you.

You have been informed as of now and forewarned. Do something with this information.

–Christopher J. Hussar, DDS, DO

 Dr. Christopher Hussar graduated from University of Michigan in 1972 with a bachelor's degree in Zoology. In 1978, he graduated from University of Detroit Dental School. His claim to fame was when he earned the Oral Pathology Award. Dr. Hussar practiced in Lansing, MI for 5 years with emphasis on TMJ and facial pain.

Seeking more knowledge to help his patients, Dr. Hussar went back to medical school and graduated from Michigan State University in 1986 with a degree in Osteopathic medicine. After a one-year internship, he began practicing medicine, and mentors along the way exposed him to chronic diseases such as Lyme and people who were ill from infections in their jaw. He specializes in diagnosing the chronically ill. Dr. Hussar is retired, but is available for consults.

Preface

Imagine your loved one was slowly dying from an undiagnosed case of stage 4 lung cancer that had spread to their bones and all of their lymph nodes. You rush them to the hospital because they are having a hard time breathing and keeping anything in, making them severely dehydrated and malnourished. You tell the ER doctor that their regular doctor just ran some blood work the day before that picked up signs of cancer, but they told your loved one that they didn't treat cancer. Actually, the doctor didn't even believe that stage 4 cancer exists!

You ask the ER doctor to please run some tests to see if your loved one does indeed have cancer. The ER doctor tells you that they don't diagnose nor treat cancer in the ER. They tell your loved one to make an appointment with an oncologist like everyone else does. The problem is they are dying, and the oncologist has a three-month waiting list.

The ER doctor gives your loved one a shot of an antidepressant and sends them home to die. What would you do? Where would you go?

Unfortunately, this is the reality for anyone that has Chronic or Late Stage Lyme Disease. Lyme disease is like cancer and AIDS; it is an immunosuppressive disease that can lead to death. It is known as the "Great Imitator" because it mimics over 350 diseases.

This is part of the reason why the #1 World Pandemic is going unrecognized and undiagnosed by the medical community.

The "Powers that Be," including Center for Disease Control (CDC), American Lyme Disease Association (ALDF), Infectious Disease Society of America (IDSA), American Medical Association (AMA), Insurance companies, Big Pharma, media, and anyone else they are in bed with, are lying to the world about what Lyme actually is. Most medical doctors deny that Chronic Lyme Disease exists, because that is what is being taught in medical schools. Medical schools use the information they receive from IDSA, which has not updated their information since 2006.[2] The CDC says Lyme disease is rare and stands behind IDSA.[3] They dictate to the medical community that two to four weeks of antibiotics will cure you. They say you can only get Lyme disease from a tick. They also state that only 10–20% of people treated for Lyme disease experience lingering symptoms of fatigue, pain, or joint and muscle aches. The CDC states that they are cured and that their symptoms are now only a side effect of having had the disease.[4]

What the "Powers that Be" are not telling you is that you don't have a bacterial infection, which sheds LPS (Lipopolysaccharide). Instead, you have something worse, a parasitic spirochete that sheds Lipoproteins (fungal antigens). When these fungal antigens or triacylated lipoproteins are scarfed up by a presumed B cell that is infected with a dormant virus like Epstein-Barr, it causes the

---

[2]   "Updated Guidelines on Diagnosis, Treatment of Lyme Disease." *IDSA*. Web. <http://www.idsociety.org/updated_guidelines_on_diagnosis_treatment_of_lyme_disease/>

[3]   @Lymenews. "CDC Stands by IDSA Lyme Treatment Guidelines | LymeDisease.org." *LymeDisease.org*. 15 Dec. 2015. Web. <https://www.lymedisease.org/cdc-stands-by-idsa/>

[4]   "Post-Treatment Lyme Disease Syndrome." *Centers for Disease Control and Prevention*. Centers for Disease Control and Prevention, 03 Nov. 2016. Web. <https://www.cdc.gov/lyme/postlds/index.html>

infected cells not to die. This is the deadly fungal–viral synergy that causes Cancer or Post-Sepsis Syndrome.

Google "National Institutes of Health (NIH) model of Post-Sepsis Syndrome (PSS)," and you will see it is a disease of immunosuppression, which parallels what the Centers for Disease Control (CDC) is calling "fungal meningitis."[5]

The "Powers that Be" are also not telling you that all vaccines can give you Post-Sepsis Syndrome.[6] They have been hiding this information from the public for a long time now. Thanks to the fake Lyme vaccine, we now have more proof and understanding of why people are getting Post-Sepsis Syndrome from any FDA-approved vaccine. Learn more about the fake LYMErix vaccine in Chapter 10.

Overcoming Lyme Disease reveals the real truth about where Lyme disease came from and provides the true case definition of what the disease really is—Relapsing Fever Spirochete. While one cannot truly get rid of Lyme disease, it can be overcome. You can live a healthy and happy life without suffering from many of the common symptoms associated with Lyme. *Overcoming Lyme Disease* tells my personal story about how my body was healed through holistic medicine and the daily things I do now to stay well. Much of the information in the book is not common knowledge. Within this book and the companion *Life Healing Handbook*, you will find inspiration, recipes, and protocols on how to detoxify your body and to how to feed it what it needs.

---

[5] <http://www.ohioactionlyme.org/wp-content/uploads/2015/03/Patients-Guide-to-NIHs-Post-Sepsis-Syndrome.pdf>

[6] "Deep Sequencing Reveals Persistence of Cell-associated Mumps Vaccine Virus in Chronic Encephalitis. - PubMed - NCBI." *National Center for Biotechnology Information.* U.S. National Library of Medicine. Web.

Before you continue to the introduction, please visit
www.OvercomingLymeDisease.com/free-handbook
to download your complimentary copy of the *Life Healing Handbook*. This fantastic handbook goes beyond the information presented in the book and provides you with additional resources to help you overcome Lyme and improve your life.

Introduction

Have you ever had symptoms come out of the blue that no one could explain?

In March of 2013, I became deathly ill after a routine dental appointment. I was told that I needed a crown re-done on a root canal tooth. The dentist removed it, fitted me for a new crown, and put a temporary one on the dead tooth. Within a few days, I could hardly function.

My symptoms came on fast. My feet turned blue as soon as I was standing, walking, or sitting in a chair. The only relief I had was when I elevated them, by either lying down or putting them up while I was sitting.

I had severe pain in my rib cage, lower back, legs and feet, along with severe cramping and pain in my abdomen. I developed horrible night sweats, which prevented me from sleeping more than an hour at a time.

I went from being able to drive my car to needing someone to drive me. I became so sensitive to touch that any piece of clothing hurt my skin and body when wearing them.

I had a hard time concentrating, and I was unable to perform daily tasks, like walking or remembering that I had the stove on. All of these symptoms are symptoms of Lyme disease and their co-infections, but I didn't know it, nor did any of my doctors!

Growing Up

I grew up poor and sick because of bad nutrition. When I was four, my parents divorced. My dad, who started off life as an A student and a great athlete, turned to alcohol and drugs after high school. He had major health issues and did not support us financially. My mom had to work three jobs to try to provide for my sister, brother, and me. We moved from place to place, every six months to a year, and at times, we had to change school districts.

We had babysitters who were physically, verbally, and sexually abusive to us. Most of the time, my sister Debbie, who was only three years older than me and one year older than my brother Richie, watched us. When we lived in Milan, Michigan, we were lucky; my dad's parents, my Grandpa and Grandma Heath, would watch us. We loved to go to their home since they had a man-made lake on their property that they opened to the public. We got to swim daily, go for walks, play beach volleyball, see lots of family and friends that would stop by, fish, and more. Grandma Heath would make us breakfast, lunch, and dinner, give us snacks, buy us clothes, and play games with us. Most importantly, she gave us the stable love that we longed for!

My dad was the second youngest of seven children. We had a huge family, with lots of cousins and distant cousins who cared for us. My mom's family was smaller, with one sibling, her generous, loving sister, Alice. Her parents divorced before I was born and had children in their new marriages, expanding her family to four half-siblings and three step-siblings.

We spent time with each set of grandparents, but mostly with my mom's mentally and physically abusive mother and her hardworking and kind stepdad. We loved going there, not for the abuse, but to be with our young aunt and uncles who were fun and like siblings to us. Regardless of my grandma's bipolar personality disorder, she provided food and shelter and took us on family trips up north to their cabin.

One of my best friends, Anita Linden, would invite me to church. I loved going and hearing how God loves each and every one of us, no matter how much money we have, or no matter what we have done, or what was done to us, for that matter. I was given the *Holy Bible* and started to read it. The stories in it touched my heart. That is when I gave my heart to the Lord at the young age of ten. I can still vividly remember to this day where I was and how I felt after asking Christ to come into my heart to be my Lord and Savior! I finally had the unconditional love that I longed for, and really, all of us do!

My mom remarried again when I was ten years old. Since we had been really poor, I didn't get to see a dentist until then. Because of my nutrient-lacking diet and poor hygiene, I had ten cavities. My dentist filled them with mercury fillings. If I didn't already have a hard time focusing in school because of poor nutrition, this toxic treatment really affected, not only my grades, but my health. Even though I was properly vaccinated, my health continued to deteriorate. I got the Mumps and Scarlet Fever. Lucky me—I was out of school for a month!

One of the last moves my mom took me on was in my in sophomore year to Ypsilanti High School, with a class size two to three times larger than Milan, where I grew up. I cried for two weeks straight in fear of being in a new school, and in sadness, missing my friends in Milan. I was one of the smallest kids in my grade. This was not good when starting new schools, I assure you, especially when you are poor. It seemed bullies liked to pick on people like me: a tiny, petite, blue-eyed and blonde-haired girl.

A Healthy Change

During this time, my mom and stepdad started selling Meadow Fresh, which included a whey-based, lactose-free milk product and protein shakes. Through this company, I slowly started to understand the importance of good nutrition. I was introduced to a world-renowned nutritionist, Virginia Easterling Jenkins, who later became my mentor and health coach.

Virginia told me about a man named Jack LaLanne, how he was small growing up and, through good nutrition and exercise with weight training, he became strong and healthy, regardless of his past poor health state. Of course, that interested me. His story was similar to mine and his results were what I desired! So, I started working out with weights, drinking protein shakes, and eating healthy.

For an elective, I took weightlifting. There was only one other girl in the class with me. The rest were all guys on the football team. I became the captain of the JV Volleyball team that year, and in my junior and senior year, I started on the Varsity team! By my senior year, the ratio of boys to girls shifted in the weightlifting classes. I had inspired girls to work out with weights, and we now had many girls in what was once an all-boys class.

Not only did my physical health improve, but so did my mental health and ability to focus. My senior year, I had a 4.0 grade point average and was Homecoming Queen! I also worked on the school newspaper and had my own monthly nutritional column called "Healthbeat."

This was the beginning of my health journey. When I stayed on my special diet, took my supplements, exercised, changed my thinking, and walked in faith, I was healthy. When I allowed daily stresses to influence my decision to stay on course, I became sick again. Basically, I have always been beginning again.

Up until recently, that was what I did. I didn't realize how important my health was until I was bedridden with Lyme disease and co-infections.

Life Before Being Diagnosed With Lyme Disease

Leading up to my diagnosis, I was very active in my children's lives. I was a stay-at-home hockey mom on my second marriage. My first husband blessed me with my beautiful daughter, Brittany. My handsome sons, Matthew and Teddy, were from my second husband.

I was also a top leader, recruiter, new business developer, and national trainer for a home-based, direct sales business that had over thirty-six thousand reps in the United States and Canada. It gave me the freedom to work around my family's life, along with money to help pay for our kids' college, family vacations, and their sports.

This company, Silpada Designs, provided me extra income to help family and friends in need, and it gave me an opportunity to empower other women by offering them this life-changing business.

God Made Our Bodies to Heal Themselves When Given the Right Environment

When I was first diagnosed with Lyme disease, I was seriously worried that I would not be able to overcome it. Not just because of how ill I was at the time, but from hearing the words, "You can't be healed," from a couple of other Chronic Lyme Disease patients who had spent hundreds of thousands of dollars on finding a cure. Like everyone with Lyme disease, you spare no expense in trying to return to a good state of health.

One couple had gone to many different doctors, like we all do, and even went to the Mayo Clinic. Of course, the Mayo couldn't help them because we all suffer from nutritional deficiencies, lack of proper nourishment from the foods we eat, water we drink, air we breathe and sunlight we get, and not pharmaceutical deficiencies. The couple informed me that Lyme and the co-infections get into every cell of your body, making it impossible to heal. They were only partially right!

Yes, Lyme and co-infections can get into every cell of your body. The good news is God made our bodies to heal themselves when given the nutritional building blocks and the environment they need. We just need to BELIEVE it and have FAITH!

I am fortunate to have been a patient of, and have worked with, many top holistic healers for the last thirty-plus years. I am blessed to have a great support system, via my faith in God and great family and friends. It is through my good and bad life experiences that I have learned to overcome just about anything.

My Experience with Lyme Disease Is Like Everyone Else's

Before you read the rest of my story in this book, I need to make a clear point here. I now understand that it is common behavior for medical doctors, family, and friends to give up on their sick patients or loved ones with Lyme disease. I see this behavior happening daily, as I am one of several caring administrators for the Lyme Disease and Co-infections group on Facebook.

Lyme disease is almost impossible to diagnose with the corrupt CDC testing guidelines and their falsified case definition. The guideline states that Lyme is an inflammation response or an arthritic "bad knee," and not the original case definition, which is a relapsing fever. Since the truth is being covered up, Lyme patients can't get the help they need and are suffering in silence. This is why the risk of suicide is high with people with Lyme, just like it was with AIDS.

Because medical doctors are being lied to about what the disease really is, they can't explain your symptoms, so they diagnose you with other diseases. Most of these diseases are due to the co-infections you get with Lyme. Lyme causes your immune system to shut down, allowing viruses to run wild, which causes ongoing new symptoms to appear. As your symptoms keep changing, everyone starts to think you are crazy, including your doctors. I have had to work on forgiving family, friends, and my past medical doctors in order to move on with my life.

The events I had to survive have made it hard to write this book. Sharing my story is not easy; it is very humbling and sometimes traumatic, but it needs to be told in order to help others.

PART ONE

Why Do I Feel Like Death?

CHAPTER 1

The Master of Disguise

"Facts do not cease to exist because they are ignored."
–Aldous Huxley

As mentioned in the introduction, a few days after a routine dental appointment in 2013, my health began to spiral downhill. I was at my youngest son Teddy's regional playoff game for his high school ice hockey team when out of the blue, I couldn't sit or stand to watch the end of the playoff game. I had to leave the ice rink to find two chairs, so I could sit and put my feet up due to poor circulation in my legs. I thought it must have something to do with the fibroid that was found growing in me nine months earlier. From the lobby of the ice rink, I called my OB/GYN. He sounded concerned and said to come in the next morning for a vaginal ultrasound.

The next morning, I went in and was told that the fibroid had doubled in size, my uterus was now prolapsed, and I had developed adenomyosis.[7] He said one day I would need a hysterectomy, but he

---

[7] Adenomyosis is a condition in which the inner lining of the uterus (the endometrium) breaks through the muscle wall of the uterus (the myometrium). Adenomyosis can cause menstrual cramps, lower abdominal pressure, and bloating before menstrual periods and can result in heavy periods. The condition can be located throughout the entire uterus or localized in one spot. (www.webmd.com/women/guide/adenomyosis-symptoms-causes-treatments)

didn't understand why my feet were blue. I was sent home, but my symptoms continued to worsen. I called my regular doctor's office, and they told me to go to the ER right away!

In the ER, they did routine blood work and some more tests, but they only came up with the diagnosis of edema—swelling of the legs and feet. They agreed that I should get a hysterectomy, and so did my regular doctor when I went and saw her the next day. So, I scheduled the hysterectomy for two weeks later and had my pre-surgical blood work done.

Based on lots of bad experiences in my past using Western or allopathic medicine, I faxed my blood work to my semi-retired holistic doctor, Rich Easterling, ND, Ph.D., who happens to be the son of Virginia Easterling Jenkins. Rich called me and said, "Jen, you have an infection or you are just getting over one, and you're anemic." He also told me that I could shrink the fibroid via enzymes, supplements, iodine, and a change in diet.

I told my OB/GYN and regular doctor what Dr. Easterling said. They laughed and said, "No, your blood work is fine and you need to have the surgery!" Since I was in so much pain, I opted for the surgery instead. Stupid me!

Iodine was in our bread supply until the 1980s, when the FDA replaced it with bromine, which causes iodine not to be absorbed in our bodies.[8] Every cell in our body needs iodine to function optimally. Without iodine, our immune systems can't function, so our bodies can't fight infections. Iodine's main job in the body is to support our endocrine glands, like our thyroid, breasts, uterus, ovaries, and prostate. With iodine, cysts do not form on these

---

[8]   Mercola, Dr. Joseph. "Avoid This If You Want To Keep Your Thyroid Healthy." *The Huffington Post.* TheHuffingtonPost.com. Web.
<http://www.huffingtonpost.com/dr-mercola/thyroid-health_b_472953.html>

glands, including our pancreas. Iodine is known to stop cancer cells from dividing and eventually killing you.

Iodine is used by our thyroid to produce hormones that activate mitochondria in our cells. When our mitochondria are not working right, we go from anaerobic metabolism (oxygen run) to a sugar fermenting metabolism, which is the perfect feeding ground for cancer.[9] By the way, fluoride is another chemical that stops iodine from being absorbed by our thyroid.

Meet Virginia Easterling Jenkins and Her Son Richard Easterling ND, PhD

Virginia was a pioneer in holistic medicine, way ahead of her time. Virginia was an RN for over twenty years and the Head Charge Nurse at Ridgewood Hospital in Ypsilanti, when she made a life-changing career move.

Virginia was a single mom of two when she went back to school to get her degree in Cosmetology. In the 60s, Virginia followed her passion and started seeing clients in her home. She named her new business after her two children, Jeanne and Richard, the J-Rich Cosmetology Clinic, Inc.

Virginia continued her education in that field when she got her degree as an esthetician. After that, she got certified in Trichology, and then she became a Certified Nutritional Consultant. She enjoyed learning about the body and helping others. When Virginia later started seeing clients from all over the world for their nutrition

---

9   "Everything You Need To Know About Iodine Webinar by Dr. Edward F. Group." *Dr. Group's Natural Health & Organic Living Blog.* 07 Sept. 2016. Web.
    <http://www.globalhealingcenter.com/natural-health/free-iodine-webinar/>

and skincare needs, she was amazed at how many of them were sensitive to chemical products. This is why she developed the Real Purity product line.

With her background in biochemistry, Virginia started using certified organic plants and herbs to formulate cosmetics and products for the hair, body, and skin. I have personally been using the products for over thirty years and love how they let my skin breathe and feel. For more information, visit RealPurity.com.

When Virginia passed away in 1995, her son, Dr. Richard Easterling, took over Real Purity and the J-Rich Clinic. Dr. Easterling got his degrees in the following: Iridology, Naturopath Dr. and Academic PhD degree in Nutritional Science from the American Holistic College of Nutrition.

Rich, like most holistic doctors, continues his education by taking ongoing courses and attending seminars to learn from other great healers. He attended a seminar that Dr. Bernard Jensen taught, which is how Virginia learned about Dr. Jensen's deep tissue cleanses. Dr. Easterling studied the late Dr. Howell's work, the doctor who discovered digestive enzymes, and worked with the man that was given his work. He has worked with and studied under Dr. George Koffeman and Dr. George Goodheart, who started the International College of Applied Kinesiology.

Dr. Easterling is semi-retired at this time. He is spending time with his grandson Zach, mentoring him in research and development for Real Purity. Although he had a long successful career helping people get well, he no longer sees patients; however, the enzymes that he uses are still available to you when you call Real Purity.

Undetected Infection

So what did Dr. Easterling notice that no medical doctor did? I have been wondering this for the last three years. Here is what I found out: My ER blood work showed that my WBC (White Blood Count) was 9.86 thou/mcL and my RBC (Red Blood Cell) was 4.28 thou/mcL. The standard range for WBC is between 4.0 and 10.0 K/UL. I was only .14 away from exceeding the so-called healthy range. Six days later when they ran my blood work again, my WBC was 5.7 thou/mcL and my RBC was 4.07 L (Low)! My WBC was barely under the maximum limit to red flag infection and dropped almost four points in six days. Hint, this is a sign of infection or one that you are getting over. My RBC was low, meaning I was anemic. If you are a doctor, please learn how to read blood work and do not just trust a lab rat.

The doctor said he removed endometriosis,[10] but it didn't show up on the pathology report. The pain got worse, and my health continued to deteriorate. I would go into my OB/GYN office and complain that something was still wrong, and they would say I was fine, it was just part of my healing.

Looking back at my blood work a day after my surgery, my WBC was high, 19.3 thou/mcL, and my RBC was low, 3.69 thou/mcL. There must have been an infection and anemia! Did my doctor say I had an infection or did anyone at the hospital catch this? Of course not! They run blood work, but don't know how to read it.

---

[10] Endometriosis is an often painful disorder in which tissue that normally lines the inside of your uterus — the endometrium — grows outside your uterus.
http://www.mayoclinic.org/diseases-conditions/endometriosis/home/ovc-20236421

A week after my surgery, I went in and demanded more blood work. The doctor's office took my body temperature to check for a fever, but it was normal. They went ahead and drew blood to check for infection. Sure enough, a day later, the doctor's office called and prescribed me an antibiotic. He said, "Take it, and in a day or two, you will be fine." That never happened. Instead, I got worse.

Let's see what my blood work looked like, shall we? Only eleven days post-op, my WBC was 15.4 (high) and RBC was 3.82 (low). How was this a sign of infection now and not the day after my surgery when my blood work was WBC 19.3 high and RBC 3.69 low? Hmm...

Did I get this from the hospital since my white blood cells were normal before I went into the hospital? According to the CDC:

> When people go to the hospital, they should not contract a preventable healthcare-associated infection (HAI). Unfortunately, HAIs affect 5 to 10 percent of hospitalized patients in the U.S. per year. Approximately 1.7 million HAIs occur in U.S. hospitals each year, resulting in 99,000 deaths and an estimated $20 billion in healthcare costs.[11]

Pretty scary stuff! 1.7 million people get infections from hospitals each year causing 99,000 deaths! I bet you know at least one person that has died from an infection they caught in the hospital.

---

[11] http://www.cdc.gov/washington/~cdcatWork/pdf/infections.pdf

One Surgery Leads to Another

On Easter morning, three days later, I called the doctor that was on call. He ordered another antibiotic for me and said by evening, I would feel much better. Instead, the pain continued to increase to where I just wanted to curl up in a ball and die! During this time, we had a family living with us while they were looking for a new home to live in. I had sent my husband and our youngest son, Teddy, and his friends to Hilton Head Island for Spring Break, a trip that I was supposed to be well enough to go on! Fortunately, our friends that were living with us made the decision that saved my life and drove me to the ER.

The Chelsea Hospital ER ran blood work and did x-rays and a CT scan. My blood work came back showing I had a major infection. The CT scan showed an abscess in my lower right side. They immediately admitted me and started me on every strong IV antibiotic they had.

The nurse asked me if I wanted to see the chaplain. I said no since I was prepared to die and knew that in heaven, I would be pain-free. Later, I regretted that decision, since I had no family or friends staying with me that night. Despite all of the antibiotics and pain meds, nothing ever touched the physical pain I was experiencing.

The next day, I was still in a lot of pain. The on-call doctor made a decision that saved my life. He scheduled surgery for the next morning. I made it through the night, but to their horrifying surprise, they discovered an infected abscess hematoma. They put a drainage tube in me to drain out the infected blood. It took four days for the blood to drain and for my intestines to start working. (Funny how they don't like sitting in infected blood.) The doctor who did my emergency surgery kept saying that my OB/GYN owed me big time! I didn't understand it at the time, until three years later when I figured out all of the errors they made in reading my blood work.

My pain continued. I was sent home with antibiotics and pain pills after six days of being hospitalized. I went back to my OB/GYN, who took me off the antibiotics. Once again, he said I was fine. I demanded more blood work to show if the infection was gone. My blood count was good, no infection, they said. They tested me for Candida; it came back high, and rightfully so, after all of the antibiotics I was on. They tested me for parasites, via a stool sample that they mailed to a lab, and it came back negative. I have later since learned that you must run the parasite test within twenty minutes after collecting your fecal matter in order for the test to come back positive. Most parasites self-digest by creating an enzyme that decomposes them. American doctors need to learn this tip if they want to help their patients.

Another Second Opinion

I then saw my regular D.O. (Doctor of Osteopathic Medicine) for a second opinion. She put me on Prilosec for the heartburn and scheduled me for an appointment with a specialist to have a minor surgical procedure to check to see if I had any blockage in my stomach.

During this time, I saw my knowledgeable chiropractor, Dr. James Koffeman, for help with the pain and to see if I had a hiatal hernia. Dr. Koffeman adjusted me and said my stomach was stuck in my esophagus, so he showed me two techniques that Dr. Easterling had taught me in the past to naturally fix it. Dr. Koffeman put me on a natural supplement of hydrochloric acid to help with the pH imbalance going on in my gut.

When I went in for the GERD procedure, my hiatal hernia was already fixed, and it did not show up as a problem during testing. So, the doctor agreed that it was a digestion issue and told me to stay on the Prilosec, which makes no sense because my body was lacking acid for proper food digestion.

When recommending this drug to patients, doctors fail to inform their patients that they can't be on it for long periods of time. The doctors are also not putting two and two together when they start seeing some of these new symptoms or adverse reactions to the drug.

Here are some of the side effects of Prilosec:

Get emergency medical help if you have **signs of an allergic reaction to Prilosec:** hives; difficulty breathing; swelling of your face, lips, tongue, or throat.

Call your doctor at once if you have:

- severe stomach pain, diarrhea that is watery or bloody;
- seizure (convulsions);
- kidney problems--urinating more or less than usual, blood in your urine, swelling, rapid weight gain; or
- symptoms of low magnesium--dizziness, confusion; fast or uneven heart rate; tremors (shaking) or jerking muscle movements; feeling jittery; muscle cramps, muscle spasms in your hands and feet; cough or choking feeling.
- Common Prilosec side effects may include:
- stomach pain, gas;
- nausea, vomiting, diarrhea; or
- headache.[12]

---

[12]　"Prilosec Uses, Dosage & Side Effects." *Uses, Dosage & Side Effects - Drugs.com.* Drugs.com. Web. <https://www.drugs.com/prilosec.html>

So funny, the common side effects of this drug are why most people take it—stomach pain and gas. Perhaps this is why they only say you should take Prilosec for no longer than fourteen days, every four months.

By the way, taking certain digestive enzymes work better than this man-made drug, and have no bad side effects. You can also eat a bite of fermented sauerkraut and drink a little of the juice before each meal to increase your gastric acid secretions.

More Surgery

I went back weekly to my OB/GYN complaining of pain. Each time, he would perform a vaginal ultrasound, and I was told, "You just have these little ovarian cysts, but you are fine."

I ended up in the ER a month later, the night before I was to fly out of town for a pampering and gift giving, "Oprah-like" trip I had earned from the direct sales company I represented, Silpada Designs. The ER doctor ran another CT scan, and also told me my pain was caused by an ovarian cyst. He asked me why the doctor didn't remove my ovaries. Needless to say, due to extreme pain, I missed the trip!

The pain continued, and I went back to OB/GYN, who said I was fine. Finally, I just gave up on doctors and suffered in pain. I went three months barely being able to eat. I survived on protein drinks, supplements, my outdoor hot tub, and a bottle of wine at night to deal with the pain.

Regardless of how I felt, I pushed on. One day late September, I tried exercising. BOOM, my insides felt like they were being ripped out with a dull knife!

Grudgingly, I went back to my OB/GYN who informed me that my cyst had grown and that I should have a laparoscopy procedure to get rid of the cyst and clean up anything else. After the procedure, my doctor informed me that my ovaries and fallopian tubes were stuck by lesions to my abdomen wall. So, he removed the lesions off my ovaries and tubes and told me that they were still healthy.

Two days later, I ended up with a double skin infection at the surgery site. I went back to see my OB/GYN, and he prescribed an antibiotic. Of course, it did not help! So, I went back and was referred to another doctor's office for them to observe and diagnose. One of the doctors said to spray hydrogen peroxide on it. The other placed me on Ciprofloxacin, a dangerous antibiotic with lots of bad side effects.[13]

Final Surgery

When I left the doctor's office, I picked up my prescription and took one pill. I then went to my Silpada event that I had scheduled. Within twenty minutes after taking the antibiotic, I started to feel lightheaded and was having a hard time breathing. When I got to the event, there were some nurses there who looked at me. They told me I was having an allergic reaction and that I needed to go to the ER. I called my husband, and he came and picked me up and took me to the University of Michigan ER, where they gave me Benadryl and placed me on a different antibiotic.

My pain subsided for two weeks after the laparoscopic surgery, only to return with a vengeance. I went back to my OB/GYN and

---

13   "Ciprofloxacin Oral: Uses, Side Effects, Interactions, Pictures, Warnings & Dosing - WebMD." *Web-MD.* WebMD. Web. <http://www.webmd.com/drugs/2/drug-7748/ciprofloxacin-oral/details#>

had another vaginal ultrasound. He told me I had a golf ball–sized cyst on one ovary and three smaller cysts on the other ovary. He then said, "See you in six months." I was horrified! I thought, "See you in six months? When I am still hurting and healing from the infections! What an idiot! I am getting a second opinion because this cannot be normal!"

I left his office and made an appointment with another OB/GYN for a second opinion. I had to cancel at the last minute because my pain became unbearable. Six days later, which happened to be Halloween, my mother-in-law drove me back to my OB/GYN. He gave me another vaginal ultrasound and told me, "Your ovaries are now bad. You need to have them removed." I asked, "How, in six days' time, could they now be bad?" His reply offered me no explanation. All he said was, "They just did." Of course, due to the pain I was in, I had the surgery four days later that removed my ovaries, tubes, and (what he told me was) more endometriosis.

The second day post-op, I was placed on an estrogen patch to help with hot flashes. Mind you, I was estrogen-dominant before my surgery. I had enough estrogen in my body to last for a while.

Right away, after placing the estrogen patch on me, I became extremely ill. So, I took it off and decided to wait a couple more days, then give it another try. When I did, I became so nauseous that I started throwing up. I immediately took the patch off and suffered again for another two days.

Still No Relief

The pain continued. "It is post-op pain," I was informed, so I sucked it up. When I went back two weeks later to have stitches removed,

I asked, "Where was the endometriosis located?" The doctor said, "No worries, I am a good doctor, and I got it all."

I went to a new OB/GYN for the rest of my follow-up appointments. She asked me, "Why did you have your ovaries removed?" I told her, "Because my ovaries were bad." She looked at me and looked at the pathology report and said, "No, they weren't bad, and you didn't have endometriosis." I was shocked, upset, and felt betrayed! I considered suing the doctor that took my ovaries!

The reason I didn't sue my doctor is because none of the attorneys that I talked with believed I had a case, because at the time I only talked about the pathology report and not the ongoing infection. I didn't realize I had Lyme and co-infections. Plus, starting and pursuing a lawsuit would cost at least $60,000 to pay for attorney fees and experts. I didn't have that kind of money. Unfortunately, you only have two years after an injury to sue your doctors for medical malpractice. Plus, once I was diagnosed with Lyme disease, I would have to prove in court that Chronic Lyme Disease exists. Gathering the type of experts needed for this is almost impossible, as you will see in Chapters 9 and 10.

Breast Cancer Scare

In December of 2013, while I was still healing from having my ovaries removed, I went in for a routine mammogram. The test showed asymmetric density in both breasts. I was called back for another mammogram and an ultrasound. It was right before the holidays, and our family was going to Copper Mountain in Colorado for Christmas.

The nurse called and said I had to come in right away. I told her, "No, I am not. I have had enough stress and surgeries this year. I will come in after I spend time with my family." When I returned, I went back in and had both procedures. Thankfully, it was just dense tissue. I was told to come back in six months, which I did. That was the last time I had a mammogram.

Instead of having a mammogram, I now do Therma-Scan. Mammograms are not accurate for women with dense breast tissue. Additionally, they can be cancer-causing due to the radiation of the x-ray. The National Cancer Institute acknowledges that "The risk of harm from this radiation exposure is low, but repeated x-rays have the potential to cause cancer...women should talk with their healthcare providers about the need for each x-ray."[14]

Dr. Easterling tried to get me to do a Therma-Scan instead of a mammogram when my doctor had found something on my breast when I was thirty-two years old. Dr. Easterling tried to explain to me the differences and why it was the better option, but that was one medical test that I didn't want to become unbrainwashed about. Instead, it took me eighteen years and becoming deathly ill to change my thinking and educate myself.

What is a Therma-Scan and how does it work? A Therma-Scan is also known as medical thermology. According to THERMA-SCAN Reference Laboratory, LLC, website:

Medical thermology is the science that derives diagnostic indications from highly detailed and sensitive infrared images of the human body.

---

[14]   "Mammograms." *National Cancer Institute*. Web.
  <https://www.cancer.gov/types/breast/mammograms-fact-sheet#q3>

Medical thermology can reveal the abnormal metabolic and blood-flow features that cause changes in the temperature of the skin that are characteristic of certain types of diseases including breast cancer.[15]

Therma-Scans can detect breast cancer, sometimes years before x-ray mammogram or an ultrasound. It is FDA approved and there is no radiation or dye in the test. The best part for women is that it is pain-free and the cost is only around $150.

Medical Marijuana

Around this time, I started using medical marijuana to deal with the pain, stress, hot flashes, and nausea. If I did have cancer, numerous studies have proven it would help.[16]

When I ate marijuana edibles, I could sleep more than an hour at a time. When I asked Dr. Easterling about it, he informed me that, "Yes, marijuana has cannabinoid in it. Our cells carry cannabinoids receptors. That is why you are getting relief from the pain, stress, nausea, and hot flashes."

It is a shame that the US government has marijuana still categorized as a Schedule 1 drug, when there is real science that proves otherwise! Cannabis helps the body maintain internal balance, or homeostasis, which is needed for attaining optimum health.

---

[15] "Frequently Asked Questions." *FAQ.* Web. <www.thermascan.com/faq>

[16] "60 Peer-Reviewed Studies on Medical Marijuana - Medical Marijuana - ProCon.org." *ProConorg Headlines.* Web. <http://medicalmarijuana.procon.org/view.resource.php?resourceID=000884>

More Diagnoses

My story goes on, doctor after doctor, specialist after specialist, five ER visits. My blood pressure elevated to 145/90- 150/100 by June, 2014. I was diagnosed with hypothyroid during an ER run. My TSH was elevated to 43! According to Dr. Easterling, healthy levels of TSH are 2-3, and mine was 40 more than that! I was placed on 50mcg of Levothyroxine in the ER. At my follow-up appointment, my doctor increased it to 100!

I had multiple x-rays (four huge calcified lymph nodes on my sternum), and MRIs (synovial cyst, bone spurs, spinal stenosis, degenerative disks, herniated disks, twisted vertebrae, and a tilted pelvis). I was diagnosed with Chronic Pain and was sent to a Fibromyalgia seminar to learn how to live with it.[17]

> Have you ever been sent to a seminar to learn how to live
> with your pain? Better yet, have you ever been told that
> everything is in your head and you need to go see a shrink?
> I promise you, you're not crazy!
> Go to my *Life Healing Handbook* at
> **www.OvercomingLymeDisease.com/free-handbook**
> to learn more about how to stay sane while fighting Lyme.

---

[17] "University of Michigan Health System." *University of Michigan Health System.* Web. <http://www.med.umich.edu/painresearch/about/workshops.html>

CHAPTER 2

Lyme Disease Is a Clinical Diagnosis

"F.E.A.R. has two meanings: 'Forget Everything and Run' or
'Face Everything and Rise.' The choice is yours."
–Zig Ziglar

In August 2014, I finally got desperate! In all actuality, I started to wise up! My husband drove me down to Indiana to see Dr. Easterling. Rich and his wife Karen had just moved from Tennessee to Indiana. I showed Rich my blood work and all of my medical reports. Rich asked if anyone tested me for Lyme disease. Well, I thought for sure they did because they tested me for Lupus, MS, and all of the other autoimmune diseases. I was wrong. No Lyme test was given.

Thankfully, Dr. Easterling had moved down to Tennessee ten years prior to my diagnosis. That is where and when he learned about Lyme disease and worked with Dr. Jill Warner, an MD who specializes in Family and Internal Medicine. Through IV hydrogen peroxide, specialized enzymes, and supplements for each of their patients' bodies, an organic diet, and change in lifestyle, they helped Lyme patients return to good health.

If you are reading this book and you are sick and don't know why, ask your doctors for copies of all the autoimmune tests they have run to see if they tested you for Lyme disease. ELISA and Western blot test are the standard infectious disease tests given, but unfortunately, they are not accurate. Furthermore, Chronic Lyme Disease causes immunosuppression and is not an autoimmune disease, it only mimics them because of the co-infections. More on all this to come.

Where Did Lyme Disease Come From?

First of all, one must remember that there is nothing new under the sun. When God created the heavens and the Earth and everything in it, He said it was good and rested. In other words, He was done with the Creation process. I am an old Earth Creationist, meaning God created the heavens and the Earth more than a few thousand years ago, more like fourteen-plus billion years ago. I used to be a Young Earth Creationist who was scared to admit that I was wrong with the translation of the Greek word, Yom, which God used in his word to describe how long creation took in the book of Genesis. Yom can be translated as a day, a year, a season, or a time period that is unspecified.

Obviously, in the first chapter of the book of Genesis, Yom meant a time period that is unspecified, since we are still in the seventh so-called "Day" or "Yom", and God hasn't created anything new since then. We are told in 1 Thessalonians 5:21, God's Word, "Prove all things; hold fast that is good."

As technology expands and more information is revealed, we need to be open to researching and deciphering what it means.

Like how at one time man thought the world was flat. To see how science and faith converge, check out www.reasons.org.

I was unaware of the information I am about to share until after I restored my health and was no longer bedridden. Focusing on the reason why I was sick was not part of my healing. Focusing on the God-given ways to heal my body was. So, don't be shocked by what you hear. Remember, anything is possible when it comes to healing our bodies.

First, let's debunk the myth or the lie that Lyme is a bacterial infection. It is not a bacterial infection! It is worse! It is a parasitic spirochete that sheds fungal antigens. It is not like normal bacteria, which sheds LPS (Lipopolysaccharides). The shedding of the fungal antigens shuts down your immune system, causing immunosuppression. Any latent virus that you may have in your body, like Epstein-Barr or herpes, gets free rein once your immune system is shut down. This can happen with any immunosuppressive disease, like AIDS or Lymphoma. This is why antibiotics don't cure Chronic Lyme Disease. It is not a bacterial infection; it is a fungal/viral synergy, like fungal meningitis.[18]

You don't see or read about this on TV or the Internet because there is a huge cover-up going on. I recommend looking into who owns the patents on Lyme disease and their tests kits. More on this to come in Chapters 9 and 10.

Where did Spirochetes come from? In an August 29, 2006, article published in *Proceedings of National Academy of Sciences of the United States of America,* by Lynn Margulis and others, Lynn shows a graph of the co-evolution of ancient bacteria called Thermophile

---

[18]   "Fungal Meningitis." *Centers for Disease Control and Prevention.* Centers for Disease Control and Prevention, 15 Apr. 2016. Web. <https://www.cdc.gov/meningitis/fungal.html>

with Spirochetes. It shows that spirochetes have been around for 500 million to 2.5 billion years and explains how they are unique phylum, ancient creators, like microbial dinosaurs.[19]

Notice, they were separate from bacteria and merged with them. Because very little is known about this so-called "bacteria", the CDC and IDSA (the ALDF front) have been able to spin this disease without the public even batting an eye.

The Strain

Have you ever seen the American drama show called *The Strain?* The next part of this story totally reminds me of it. The show is about the head doctor at the CDC's New York–based Canary Project, a rapid response team, who discovers a rare viral outbreak that has similarities to an ancient strain of vampirism.

Instead of biting you with sharp teeth and drinking your blood, those infected with the strain would become zombie-like and they would bite you with their lizard-like tongue, spreading a parasite or strain that would turn you into one of them. Actually, the rare "virus" came from Germany to America, via someone with lots of money, political strings and influence, in order to help himself heal from a deadly disease.

In order to go under the radar, the head vampire and his followers put a virus in the communication system of everyone in New York that made their phones, internet, and media obsolete.

---

19 "The Last Eukaryotic Common Ancestor (LECA): Acquisition of Cytoskeletal Motility from Aerotolerant Spirochetes in the Proterozoic Eon." *The Last Eukaryotic Common Ancestor (LECA): Acquisition of Cytoskeletal Motility from Aerotolerant Spirochetes in the Proterozoic Eon.* Web. <https://www.omicsonline.org/references/the-last-eukaryotic-common-ancestor-leca-acquisition-of-cytoskeletal-motility-from-aerotolerant-spirochetes-in-the-proterozoic-eon-901283.html>

Obviously, that helped the strain gain ground and infect more people. The show goes on with the CDC doctor trying to contact the rest of the world to warn them and prevent the strain from taking over mankind.

Let's talk similarities, shall we? The Germans were the first to discover the "bacteria" that causes Lyme disease in the late 1800s.[20] They used it for biological warfare and so did other countries, like Japan.

After World War II, the US brought over the Nazi's lab chief, Erich Traub. Traub shared the information, helping to create the groundwork for Fort Detrick's offshore germ warfare animal disease lab on Plum Island. It explains why Lyme disease has become more prevalent. The US government was working on this biological (germ) weapon. Unfortunately, they must not have realized how dangerous this parasitic fungal-like antigen mixed with animal viruses was to humans—or did they? They didn't realize that tick- or flea-infested birds or deer could carry it off the island into Lyme, Connecticut. That is where the "bacteria" that causes Lyme got its name.[21] See Chapter 10 for more details.

By the way, this information is hard to come by because the "Powers that Be" don't want this information known. This is where the real story and the show *The Strain* are not similar. On the show, the CDC was the good guy. As you start to connect the dots, you will see why the CDC has a lot to lose if the real truth about Lyme disease is exposed.

---

[20]   "History of Lyme Disease | Bay Area Lyme Foundation." *Bay Area Lyme Foundation*. Web. <http://www.bayarealyme.org/about-lyme/history-lyme-disease/>

[21]   "Plum Island, Lyme Disease And Operation Paperclip - A Deadly Triangle." *Plum Island, Lyme Disease And Operation Paperclip - A Deadly Triangle*. Web. <http://www.rense.com/general67/plumislandlyme.htm>

How Does One Get Lyme Disease?

First of all, you can be born with Lyme disease. I truly believe that I may have been born with it or I got infected early in life. When I was in first or second grade, I had a weird thing happen. I had what looked like a tip of a lead pencil on top of my middle right-hand knuckle. Within a week or two, an infection grew there and it was full of pus, with a round, red, growing margin around. During school one day, my teacher sent me to the school nurse to look at it. The nurse thought that maybe it was from me being accidently stabbed by a lead pencil, but was perplexed because she had never seen anything like that before. She surgically removed the black tip from my knuckle and opened up the wound to drain the pus. She then put a topical antibiotic on it followed by a bandage to cover up the whole infected area. Sometime after that, the infection cleared up.

I remember struggling really hard in school to read and keep up with the rest of the class, and at times, I would fall asleep during class. This is when my mom hired a tutor to teach me skills on how to learn and read. Regardless, I always had a hard time focusing in school, unlike the rest of the kids in my class. I started having headaches and joint aches. It was during this time that my mom took me to my first chiropractor for help and treatments.

In my early twenties, I fell at work. I had twisted all of the vertebrae in my neck and upper back. My ligaments and muscles that attached my ribs to the sternum stretched, causing my ribs to go out of place. It caused major pain in my chest, and I had shooting pain down my arm caused by nerve pinching in my chest. I had a sprained rotator cuff and had bruised my inner upper arm to the bone.

I went to an Urgent Care nearby for treatment. They took an x-ray of my chest. It showed I had four calcified lymph nodes in my sternum. The doctors concluded that I must have had a major infection at one point in my life for the lymph nodes to have calcified. Calcification is one of our body's natural defenses to stop foreign invaders. It does this when cancer is present, as well.

When my mom was seventeen years old, before she had children, she was hospitalized with hepatitis, anemia, pancreatitis, and renal disease. My dad started having heart attacks in his thirties, along with congestive heart failure. Both his parents died of heart issues.

As a child, I was sick all the time and suffered from chronic bronchitis. I remember being on antibiotics because of it. With Lyme mimicking over 350 diseases, I could have gotten Lyme in many ways. My mom could have passed it on to me during birth or I could have gotten it from an insect bite.

I am lucky because my body produces antibodies to Borrelia burgdorferi, the "bacteria" that causes Lyme. Not sure how long I have had Lyme, but before I fell deathly ill, I was able to stay well from the natural antibodies my body was producing, watching my diet and taking special supplements and enzymes.

I believe I went septic or post-sepsis when my crown was taken off my infected root canal. The amount of infection being dumped into my body via my infected root canal was too much for my body to handle. The antibodies I was producing more than likely forced the spirochete to go into cyst form. It would be interesting to know if this is why cysts kept growing on my ovaries or if it was because I was iodine deficient, or both.

The spirochete changes into three forms to avoid the body's immune system: the shape of a spirochete, L-form that is cell wall deficient, and cyst form. The spirochete could have gone into hiding, not only in my ovaries, but also on my lower spine. Via MRI, I was diagnosed with having a Synovial Cyst on my spine only two weeks after the teeth cleaning of an infected tooth that had a crown removed from it that sent the infection throughout my body.

Other Ways to Get Lyme Disease

Any insect that bites can give you Lyme disease and co-infections. The CDC says only ticks can give you Lyme. Unfortunately, they are aware that it is more than ticks that can give you the Post-Sepsis Syndrome outcome. The CDC has not updated the information that they share with the public or doctors on Lyme disease since 2006. They still are saying ticks only![22]

The truth is, Lyme can be transmitted by the bite of not only ticks, but mosquitoes, biting flies, spiders, lice, bed mites, and more. This is why a lot of people are walking around asymptomatic, or have been diagnosed with other diseases, not knowing they are infected. The Dr. Jones Kids website provides this information:

> At least nine species of ticks, six species of mosquitoes, 13 species of mites, 15 species of flies, two species of fleas, and numerous wild and domestic animals (including rabbits, rodents, and birds) have been found to carry the spirochete that causes Lyme disease. (Lyme disease symptoms may appear days, weeks, months or years after initial infection).[23]

[22] "Transmission." Centers for Disease Control and Prevention. Centers for Disease Control and Prevention, 04 Mar. 2015. Web. <https://www.cdc.gov/lyme/transmission/index.html>

[23] "Dr Jones Kids." *Dr Jones Kids*. Web. <https://sites.google.com/site/drjoneskids/home>

Ninety percent of Lyme genes are unrelated to any bacteria known to man, making it one of the most complex bacteria.[24] Since the proper blood test to check for Lyme is not used, you can also get it through a blood transfusion and organ donations.

The website TruthAboutLymeDisease.com shares:

> Lyme literate doctors are learning Lyme may be transmitted sexually, through saliva, organ donations, blood transfusions and passed to your children congenitally. Fleas, mosquitoes and other blood sucking insects can also carry Lyme Disease. These insects feed on any animals, deer, mice, birds, etc., pick up bacterias then feed on you. It is not uncommon for an entire household to test positive for Lyme, unlikely will two people have identical symptoms. There are varying degrees from functional to bedridden.[25]

According to Dr. Christopher Hussar, "Insects become infected themselves from contaminated blood with multiple critters (co-infections) from feeding on contaminated animals and then feed on you."

The most controversial way you could have gotten Lyme disease is if you were in the fake/failed LYMErix vaccine trial. More on this in Chapter 10.

The United States CDC says that there are 300,000 new cases of Lyme disease a year in the US. But thanks to the CDC crime of changing the case definition and testing for the disease (in 1994

24   Porcella, Stephen F., and Tom G. Schwan. "*Borrelia Burgdorferi* and *Treponema pallidum*: a comparison of functional genomics, environmental adaptations, and pathogenic mechanisms." *Journal of Clinical Investigation.* American Society for Clinical Investigation, 15 Mar. 2001. Web. <https://www.ncbi.nlm.nih.gov/pmc/articles/PMC208952/>

25   "TruthAboutLymeDisease." *TruthAboutLymeDisease.com.* Web. <http://www.truthaboutlymedisease.com/>

during the Dearborn Conference) to sell a fake vaccine and testing kits, that number only represents 15% of the cases being reported. In the original testing for Lyme, you only needed IgM or IgG antibodies of 41-kD (the anti-flagellar antibody) plus the triad of symptoms to prove you had Lyme disease.

In "Antigens of Borrelia Burgdorferi Recognized during Lyme Disease Appearance of a New Immunoglobulin M Response and Expansion of the Immunoglobulin G Response Late in the Illness," CDC officer Alan Steere, who helped with this crime, explains how you only need 41-kD on your Western blot to prove you have Lyme disease. This is eight years before the Dearborn Conference where he and other corrupt CDC officers decided on an altered criterion for it to be positive which makes it almost impossible to get diagnosed.

This observation suggests that the 41-kD antigen of B.burgdorferi may give better results in an ELISA for early Lyme disease than the current test, which uses sonicated whole spirochetes (11, 12). Furthermore, in this study, IgM antibodies to the 41-kD polypeptide were usually apparent by immunoblots before IgM titers were elevated by the current ELISA.[26]

The FDA validated a new test that was even better than this test. The test was specific for recombinant fragment of Borrelia burgdorferi flagellin. In 1992, Yale University (patent owners for the fake LYMErix vaccine) applied for a patent and was approved in 1997 for this trusted FDA method: U.S. patent 5,618,533.[27] Of course, this test is not used, thanks to the Dearborn Stunt that will be discussed in Chapter 10.

---

[26]   https://www.ncbi.nlm.nih.gov/pmc/articles/PMC423723/pdf/jcinvest00109-0086.pdf

[27]   Flavell, Richard A., Erol Fikrig, Robert Berland, and Yale University. "Patent US5618533 - Flagellin-based Polypeptides for the Diagnosis of Lyme Disease." *Google Books.* 10 Dec. 1993. Web. <https://www.google.com/patents/US5618533?

Because of this crime against humanity, 85% of people with Lyme disease are not being reported! Can you see why this is the #1 World Pandemic? So, what is the real number of people infected with Lyme each year in the US? It could be up to 2,000,000 people! According to recent research from UCSF, half of them will become disabled, with or without any medical treatments.[28] Out of these forgotten disabled victims, only a few may ever get disability because the real disease is not being recognized as what the disease it really is.

Did you notice that the UCSF study said that half of Lyme patients will become disabled, with or without medical treatment? So no matter what, if you take antibiotics or not, you may become disabled. The question is, why are only half the people becoming disabled? Perhaps it has something to do with their immune system and their body's ability to fight chronic infection. There is no research on this, so we don't know. I think we need to start looking at the lifestyle and genetic background of those that are not disabled to find some answers. More on the CDC crime in Chapter 10.

There is another good book out there, *Cell Wall Deficient Forms: Stealth Pathogens* by Lida Holmes Mattman, which was published in 1974. Lida believed that everyone in the US has been infected with Lyme. Of course, depending on how much OspA (fungal antigen) you are exposed to from Lyme and what co-infections you have, like Babesia, everyone develops different symptoms.[29]

---

[28] "Lyme Disease May Be Diagnosable via Transcriptome Signature | GEN Genetic Engineering & Biotechnology News - Biotech from Bench to Business." *GEN*. Web. <http://www.genengnews.com/gen-news-highlights/lyme-disease-may-be-diagnosable-via-transcriptome-signature/81252365>

[29] Mattman, Lida H. *Cell Wall Deficient Forms: Stealth Pathogens*. Boca Raton: CRC, 2001. Print.

Clinical Diagnosis

The number one way to diagnose Lyme disease and its co-infections, since the crime against humanity at Dearborn, is now through a clinical observation based on your symptoms. By the way, changing symptoms were a sign of Lyme disease before the Dearborn stunt, but are no longer allowed to prove you have Lyme because they changed the case definition to only an arthritic "bad knee."[30]

In the book *Learn How the Top 20 Alternative Doctors in America Can Improve Your Health*, Dr. Edward Kondrot interviewed twenty doctors. According to Dr. Lee Cowden, a leading Holistic Lyme Specialist who Dr. Kondrot interviewed, Lyme disease mimics over 350 diseases.[31] If you have been diagnosed with Fibromyalgia, Chronic Fatigue Syndrome, Migraine Headaches, Insomnia, Anxiety, Depression, Dementia, Autism, ADHD, Multiple Sclerosis, Rheumatoid Arthritis, Parkinson's Disease, Lou Gehrig's disease, or Alzheimer's disease, just to name a few, I suggest you second guess your doctor.

Another test that is not FDA approved to check for Lyme disease is using the Darkfield (Live Blood) Microscopy blood test. According to Aqua Technology:

> You may find it difficult to locate many medical doctors that use this technique. The FDA does not approve of Darkfield microscopic blood analysis, therefore many doctor's hands are tied. Viewing a fresh, natural blood sample (a sample not altered

---

[30] http://www.ohioactionlyme.org/wp-content/uploads/2015/03/Patients-Guide-to-NIHs-Post-Sepsis-Syndrome.pdf

[31] Kondrot, Edward, and Abram Ber. *Learn How the Top 20 Alternative Doctors in America Can Improve Your Health*. Charleston, SC: Advantage, Member of Advantage Media Group, 2014. Print.

with any stains, etc., needed for normal microscopic exams), under the technology of a dark field microscope, will reveal conditions of your blood not normally even considered during the diagnosis of a normal blood test performed in doctor's office or a lab.

However, an increasing number of health professionals have found that the use of this technique allows inspection of cellular dynamics which as noted above normally escape analysis or diagnosis using orthodox medical tests.[32]

Imagine that, the FDA does not approve of this method! By the way, it can take anywhere from hours, days, or weeks for the all of the parasites and spirochetes to flee the red blood cells and make themselves known. Just like you need to grow the culture for strep throat, you need to give this test time to show you are infested.

But wait! Check out this double standard when testing for another spirochete disease called Syphilis. "The definitive method for diagnosing syphilis is visualizing the spirochete via Darkfield microscopy. This technique is rarely performed today because it is a technologically difficult method."[33] What? How can it be a technologically difficult method if it can be performed at your doctor's office or at a lab? I am sure the degree of mistakes can't possibly be worse than the poor testing they are using now.

---

[32]   "Darkfield Microscopy, Live Blood Cell Analysis." *Darkfield Microscopy, Live Blood Cell Analysis.* Web. <https://www.aquatechnology.net/darkfield.html>

[33]   "Syphilis - CDC Fact Sheet (Detailed)." *Centers for Disease Control and Prevention.* Centers for Disease Control and Prevention, 17 Nov. 2016. Web. <https://www.cdc.gov/std/syphilis/stdfact-syphilis-detailed.htm>

It can be incredibly difficult to get an accurate diagnosis for Lyme Disease, but you can start to identify symptoms and get the support you need. For a copy of a Lyme Symptom Checklist, go to my *Life Healing Handbook* at **www.OvercomingLymeDisease.com/free-handbook**.

CHAPTER 3

Where Do You Go For Help?

"If you are not your own doctor, you are a fool."
—Hippocrates – founder of Medicine

When I got back in town from seeing Dr. Easterling, I contacted my doctor at the Ann Arbor Spine Center and asked her to run a blood test for Lyme disease. She agreed to order the test, but she informed me that she does NOT treat Lyme disease. I said, "No problem, I just need the test ordered."

Searching for a doctor who could figure out what was going on with my health, I had switched my main medical doctor right before this test came back. My new doctor ordered a colonoscopy and an abdominal ultrasound. Everything looked fine. When the ELISA, or Lyme Antibody Test, came back 1.38 (high), she started me on antibiotics and put me on an anti-anxiety pill.

Like Kryptonite is to Superman, Mold Is to a Lyme Patient!

The next test to confirm Lyme disease, according to the CDC, is the Western blot test. So, my doctor ordered what was "supposed to be" a Western blot test. I had my blood drawn and went up to Drummond Island for my daughter's destination wedding.

I was feeling pretty good, for me, on the car ride up to Drummond Island. When I got to our cabin, I noticed a type of black mold in the master suite bathroom and on the master bedroom windows in the building. I went from being able to eat and feeling pretty good to being unable to function.

I could barely make it to any of the events, and I was only able to attend her wedding and the beginning toast at her wedding reception. It was a beautiful wedding, but I was too sick to really be a part of it. My friend, Kim Ellicott, and cousin, Kimberly Honan, had to literally dress me and walk me to the ceremony start line, which was right outside my cabin. My husband and youngest son Teddy had to hold me close, so I wouldn't fall as we walked down the outdoor steps to the wedding site!

What was supposed to be one of the happiest days in my life, seeing my daughter marry the man of her dreams, turned out to be one of my darkest moments. I wasn't able to be truly present because I was so ill and certain family and friends thought I had gone crazy and that I was faking my symptoms. Yes, I know what pain and hurt feel like.

CDC Cover-Up

While I was at my daughter's wedding in the Upper Peninsula of MI, Washtenaw County CDC called me and left a message to call them back. I thought to myself, "Wow, they must know that Lyme is in our area, and they are calling to give me a name of a doctor that can help me." WRONG! Instead, they asked me, "Have you traveled outside of Washtenaw County in the last two years?"

"What?" I asked.

"Have you ever traveled outside Washtenaw County?" they asked me again. Totally perplexed, I said, "Of course, I have!"

"Well then, you could have gotten it from another county," was their response.

I was angry and floored by their ignorance, and so I challenged them! I then asked, "What doctors can I see? All of my doctors are telling me they don't treat Lyme disease."

They responded, "You will have to get in with an Infectious Disease Doctor."

"Can you help me get in?"

"We don't do that. You will need to talk to your primary care doctor."

Angry and upset, I hung up the phone! I thought to myself, "Really, why did they even call! Obviously, they don't want to acknowledge that Lyme is in our area!" I also fretted, "What doctor will see me right away and help me?"

Two days later, Tuesday, August 19th, 2014, I had a bone scan done. My caring specialist, Dr. Steward at the Ann Arbor Spine Center, waited to order the test because she was worried about the radiation from the bone scan, since I had had numerous MRIs, CT scans, and x-rays. She was concerned about the four huge calcified lymph nodes on my sternum and didn't want the bone scan to grow anything else.

"We Don't Diagnose or Treat Lyme Disease in the ER"

On Wednesday, August 20th, four days after the wedding, I saw a female neurologist at St. Joseph Hospital. She concurred that if my Western blot test came back positive, then I had Lyme disease. Unfortunately, the Western blot was never ordered because the CDC failed to tell doctors that Lyme was in the area or inform them about how to order a Western blot test.

Instead, a second Lyme Antibody test was ordered, and it came back at 1.33 (high) on Thursday, August 21st. That same day, my heart palpitations and breathing were so bad, I ended up in the ER again. They gave me an hour of IV fluids and took a chest x-ray. I was asked if I had ever been diagnosed with emphysema. I told them no, and I was in need of the proper test, the Western blot test, to rule out Lyme disease.

The young and ignorant ER doctor informed me that they do not diagnose nor treat Lyme in the ER, and I needed to make an appointment, like everyone else, with an infectious disease doctor. I was given an antidepressant (which happened at every ER visit) and sent home with my high blood pressure and trouble breathing.

When I got home from the ER, I called my doctor's office and informed them about what had happened. I asked if they could order the Western blot test, and they said, "Yes, come in and pick up the order."

The Common Medical Doctor Chant, "I Don't Treat Lyme Disease"!

I had a follow-up appointment with my doctor at the spine clinic to go over my bone scan that Thursday, but had to miss it since I ended up in the ER. She called me with the results and was very concerned. The bone scan showed an acute versus subacute right approximate sixth rib fracture. It also showed the four huge calcified lymph nodes on my sternum. She asked if anyone was watching them to see if they grow. I told her no. She then suggested for me to have them monitored.

I thanked her for calling and told her I was going to get a Western blot test done the next day to rule out Lyme disease. She said great, but she does NOT treat Lyme disease. I must say, this did not surprise me by now. I was hearing the same chant over and over again by all of my medical doctors. I now know why! You can't treat Lyme with man-made medicine, and there is a huge cover-up going on!

The next day, my friend Lynn, who happened to be the wife of the Vice President of Chelsea Hospital, picked me up to take me to get my script and have my blood drawn. When I reached my doctor's office, winded, of course, the receptionist informed me that the doctor on call had said, "Don't be too excited if you have Lyme disease. It is nothing to be excited about!"

I told her, "Thanks, but I just need to know what is going on in my body so I can treat it." I grinned and left. My thoughts were, "Really! Like I want this disease?!"

Wrong Blood Test Ordered

Whoever said, "Third time's a charm," has never walked in my shoes. On my way to the lab, I read the orders. No, I am NOT a doctor, but by now I know what the same blood order looks like! Yes, once again, the other doctor ordered me the Lyme Antibody Test! I questioned the lab, and they concurred. But to my amazement, they didn't know what a Western blot test was! After twenty minutes of them making calls, I believe one was to the CDC, they told me they knew what to do.

I got my blood drawn and was told I would know in five to six business days. Later that day, I received two phone calls from my doctor's office informing me that, "We do NOT treat Lyme disease, and if the test came back positive, it is NOT accurate. The ONLY accurate test for Lyme disease is the IGeneX test. You will have to call this 800 number to order it. When you get the test, bring it into the office and we will draw your blood and mail it in for you. But you need to come in on a Monday, Tuesday or Wednesday for the draw. The test needs to get to the IGeneX lab in California, before the weekend, for accurate testing." My doctor's office called me on Monday, Tuesday, and Wednesday to inform me that they do not treat Lyme disease. See why I was in shock! By the way, the IGeneX test is not FDA approved. Imagine that!

I looked up the test, and it was anywhere from $500–$1,000! Since I didn't know which one to order, I decided to wait. On Friday, August 22nd, the same day of my blood draw, I took the last antibiotic I had and started throwing up for over a week straight.

Thank God for Good Friends!

An angel showed up on Tuesday, August 26th. Her name is Julie Wash, a caring, loving friend of mine. Like most parents, you become best friends with your kid's friend's parents. Her fun-loving daughter, Ashleigh, was my daughter's maid of honor.

Julie stopped by to turn in her Silpada party orders. I was in bed fighting to breathe when she arrived at our house. She was shocked that my mom, stepdad, and husband were outside, acting as though life was as usual, while I was upstairs in bed, alone and suffering. I asked Julie to make me potassium broth from the ingredients my mom and stepdad picked up for me the day before. She graciously did and literally had to spoon-feed me the broth. I was too weak to feed myself. Unfortunately, I ended up throwing up the broth too. I couldn't keep anything in me.

Who Can Help Me?

The next morning, after suffering for five days with extreme hunger, unable to eat or drink anything because it felt like it was stuck in my throat, and vomiting, I asked my husband to call the doctor's office. My hot flashes had increased to every fifteen minutes, followed by severe bone chills. I was unable to sleep. I had pain throughout my body and high blood pressure, along with a racing pulse while lying down. When I stood up, my blood pressure dropped.

When my husband handed me his phone, I told the on-call doctor that I just had thrown up three times in a row. My husband right away told the doctor that I had not thrown up! I was in disbelief! How could he have said that? He didn't see me throw up because he was sleeping in another room.

The on-call doctor told me that he doesn't know me and I should go to the ER. I told him I was just at the ER five days ago, and they sent me home. I asked him if I could come into the office to see him that morning, and he replied, "I have my patients. I don't have any time to see you, plus I don't treat Lyme disease!" Unbelievable! Here I am pleading for my life, and he tells me he can't see me!

I hung up the phone, and in a panic, I called Dr. Easterling. Rich found the Born Clinic, a holistic clinic for me in Grand Rapids, that he felt could help. Rich put a call in first to refer me. I then made my call and they offered me an appointment that day. Wow! Talk about service! My husband left for work, angry with me for still throwing up; he was totally against me going to the Born Clinic. Since I was too weak to drive myself, I picked an appointment two days later in hopes that someone could drive me, or hopefully, I would be well enough to drive myself.

Call It God or Your Intuition!

During this week of throwing up nonstop, I lived in our master suite. Since I was too weak to go down to the kitchen, I had a coffee machine in my bathroom to make coffee for my coffee enemas. The coffee enemas helped with my pain and my brain fog. After my coffee enemas, I took Epsom salt baths with essential oils, ginger baths, or apple cider vinegar baths. I would praise God by worshiping Him through Christian music on Pandora. Worshiping God took my focus off of my pain and suffering. It was the only time I felt my physical and emotional pain subside. Regardless of the moments of relief and comfort, I prayed that God would just let me die.

It was during this time that I felt God speak to me and say, "You aren't going to die!" (If you don't believe in God, call it your Intuition). The small voice in me nudged, "You aren't going to die. You are going to figure out what is wrong with you. You will get better, and you will help others with all of the knowledge you have obtained over the years."

I truly had a peace deep down in my soul that I was going to survive and that God wanted to use me for His glory. Isaiah 53:5 kept coming to my mind, "But he was pierced for our transgressions, he was crushed for our iniquities; the punishment that brought us peace was upon him, and by his wounds, we are healed." God had already paid the price and created two futures, one that I was currently living and the other was there for the asking by faith.

If you are reading this and feel hopeless, I assure you are not alone. Don't let your current situation determine your destiny. Focus on the positives in your life and believe that you can get better.

The Born Clinic

On Friday, August 29th, 2014, I miraculously made the drive to my appointment at the Born Clinic. What should have taken an hour and forty-five minutes took me three hours, since I had blurry vision and had to stop and throw up along the way a couple of times.

Dr. Coller examined me, asked me lots of questions, and then ordered blood work. He was going to run a Candida test, but I already had one done with my other doctors, and it was high. He then ordered a food allergies test, since everything I was eating or drinking wasn't staying down. Dr. Coller gave me the Lyme Disease Follow-Up Check List and then said, "Let's do a Zyto test on you to see what it picks up. For now, we will start you on liquid silver for the Candida, and let's give you some IV nutrition today."

With tears in my eyes, I told him, "Thank you!"

"Finally," I thought, "a knowledgeable doctor that knows what Lyme disease is and realizes that I am really sick, and he isn't afraid to help me!"

Dr. Coller was going to give me some vitamins for my body when I shared with him that I was planning on taking the Endo-met supplements I had gotten after having a hair analysis in June. Dr. Easterling had ordered the hair analysis from ARL (Analytical Research Labs, Inc.) for me back in January, but I didn't mail in my hair sample until the end of May.

When I received the supplements in June, I had just ended up in the ER and was diagnosed with hypothyroid. When I went to the endocrinologist, she asked me not to take any of the supplements for now, while she was ruling out thyroid cancer and Hashimoto's. The hair analysis picked up the thyroid issue and other health issues that the other regular medical doctors and specialists did not pick up.

I showed Dr. Coller the six supplements that Dr. Easterling had put me on a couple of weeks earlier: Vera-Thera CF, Cytozyme -THY, Lauricidin, and the enzymes I was on. Dr. Coller agreed that all were a good start.

Hair Analysis Is a Good Place to Start

It is hard to find a doctor who can read blood work correctly or know about nutrition. One great tool to use in figuring out what your nutritional deficiencies are is a hair analysis. Ask your doctor or holistic doctor to order you a Hair Tissue Mineral Analysis, from Analytical Research Labs, Inc. in Phoenix, AZ for extra insight as to what is going on in your body. The following information is from the personal booklet that you receive from ARL Labs, Inc. with the explanation of your hair analysis:

A hair tissue mineral analysis (HTMA) is a screening test that measures the levels of twenty-one minerals and toxic metals present in a sample of hair. Minerals are the "spark plugs" of life and play many important health related roles within the human body. Providing a "window into the cells", hair makes an excellent biopsy material and reveals a clear record of mineral metabolism. Hair, like all other body tissues, contains minerals that are deposited as the hair grows. Although hair is dead, the minerals remain as the hair continues to grow. The minerals and toxic metals are locked inside the hair during the growth stage as the body uses it for the storage and elimination of minerals.

A hair tissue mineral analysis reflects long term metabolic activity as it measures an average of mineral accumulation over a three-month period of time. This is often an advantage as the test results are not influenced by day-to-day variations in body chemistry due to stress, diet or other factors. Creating a blueprint of one's individual biochemistry, a hair tissue mineral analysis can assist in identifying mineral patterns which may be associated with stress, blood sugar and carbohydrate imbalances, metabolic rate, biochemical energy production, and glandular imbalances. Hair tissue mineral analysis is used to measure environmental contamination with toxic metals in the soil, plants and human and animal populations.[34]

---

[34] "Balancing Body Chemistry Through Hair Tissue Mineral Analysis!" *ARL Mineral Information*. Web. <http://www.arltma.com/>

A good doctor will do whatever they can do to help you. A regular MD, more than likely, will not order this test because they weren't taught more than an hour of nutrition in medical school. Ask your chiropractor, naturopathic doctor, biological dentist or DO to order one for you.

As you learned in this chapter, a healthy environment is essential when overcoming Lyme. Mold made my symptoms worse and prevented me from truly enjoying my own daughter's wedding. Learn more about making sure your home environment is healthy by getting your copy of my *Life Healing Handbook* at **www.OvercomingLymeDisease.com/free-handbook.**

CHAPTER 4

Lyme Disease: The 21st Century Plague that is Being Ignored

"For our struggle is not against flesh and blood, but against the authorities, against the powers of this dark world and against the spiritual forces of evil in the heavenly realms."
–EPHESIANS 6:15

After my IV nutrition at the Born Clinic, I saw Jordan DeJonge for diagnostic testing with the Zyto Scan. It is a hand cradle device with electrode sensors in it. You put your hand on this cradle, which is attached to a computer. The test runs for forty-five minutes to see what the automated galvanic skin response picks up.[35]

Jordan actually has Lyme disease and his dad, the late Dr. Robert DeJonge, was a Lyme-literate doctor who traveled all over the world to educate doctors on Lyme disease. Pretty interesting that over twenty years ago, he was talking about Lyme being in MI, when the CDC keeps saying it is rare. I finally was at a facility that cared about helping me and others!

---

[35] "How a Scan Works." ZYTO *Scanning Process - Learn How a Scan Works*. Web. <https://www.zyto.com/learning/howascanworks/>

Jordan ran the Zyto and it picked up not only Lyme but, based on his findings, the number one thing in me was flukes. I didn't know what a fluke was, so Jordan told me they were a type of parasite. Jordan then asked if I lived in Detroit and did I have a Michigan basement. I was perplexed and said no. He thought it was odd how much mold was being detected in me.

Jordan then mentioned one of my co-infections was Babesia, a malaria-like parasite infection. Babesia causes air hunger, day/night sweats, body chills, cough, digestive issues, and more. Those were some of the same symptoms I was experiencing. According to the CDC, it can also lead to death![36] So why aren't doctors being trained about this parasite?

The CDC, insurance companies, and most medical doctors look at the Zyto machine as quackery. Perhaps they don't want people to know what their real problems are. Dr. Lee Cowden and other top holistic doctors, like Dr. Kondrot, have been using this device to help aid in treating their patients for years.

Jordan DeJonge helped upload the Zyto with over nine thousand different frequencies. With all of the knowledge Jordan learned from his father, the device is amazing at helping to detect what is going on in your body.

I have personally bought my own Zyto hand cradle and have tested remotely with Jordan. I have had friends do remote tests with Jordan, and they are amazed at what it was able to pick up in them. Unfortunately, Jordan no longer works for the Zyto company and he is no longer at the Born Clinic.

---

[36] "Disease." *Centers for Disease Control and Prevention.* Centers for Disease Control and Prevention, 05 Feb. 2014. Web. <https://www.cdc.gov/parasites/babesiosis/disease.html>

Based on the findings, Dr. Coller scheduled my next appointment for Tuesday, September 2nd, 2014 to have another IV nutrition, Zyto, and to get my blood drawn for the IGeneX test.

Out of fear, it took me four days to look at a photo of a fluke on the Internet. I had been taking pictures with my phone of these weird aliens that were coming out of my body each time I threw up or went to the bathroom. When I overcame my fear and looked anyway, I was horrified and amazed at the same time. The photo of flukes looked exactly like the things that were coming out of me.

FLUKE WORM WITH LOTS OF EGGS !!

NOTE THE 8 DOTS WITHIN THE MOTHER

7/8/2000

(http://curezone.com/upload/_a_forums/ask_mh/fluke_worm_with_eggs_copy.jpg)

What is a fluke? According to Pinnacle Health & Wellness:

The fluke parasite is a parasitic flatworm that can cause significant health conditions in the lungs and digestive tract of the human host. This fluke or trematode refers to the suckers on the outside of its body that are used to deplete valuable nutrients from their host. These parasitic organisms initially use up the nutrients from the respiratory tract and the digestive tract causing serious health problems and then migrate to the rest of the body.

Humans can contract the fluke parasite by eating uncooked fish, vegetables, fruits and meat which has been exposed to fluke infested water. The fluke flatworm will usually set up shop in the small intestine, grow in numbers and then make their way to the rest of the body via the bloodstream and lymphatic system. Other types of these parasites can infect the liver and ingest all of the bile, when this happens the human host will not be able to digest and absorb fat in the diet.

These flatworms infect 300 million people every year mostly in Asia but has recently increased incidence in the United States. The most common types of flukes are:

1. Intestinal Fluke- this flatworm lives in the small intestine causing numerous digestive issues.

2. Liver Fluke- this species actually eats your liver and blood causing problems with fat metabolism and systemic inflammation.

3. Blood Fluke- causes infection in the blood that can cause fever and also can spread throughout the bloodstream to affect other organs and glands of the body.

4. Lung Fluke- causes irritation and inflammation in the upper respiratory tract; symptoms closely mimic that of a bacterial or viral infection.

The adult liver fluke can produce over 25,000 eggs per day. Chronic infection by this flatworm can lead to the liver disease fascioliasis. Symptoms of this fluke parasite include:

1. Vomiting
2. Stomach aches
3. Fever
4. Heightened immune response by increasing white blood cells
5. Diarrhea
6. Muscle aches and pains
7. Swelling
8. Intestinal blockage[37]

Let's look at this, shall we? They start in your lungs and intestines and then move to other body parts. Check! At least three hundred million people get infected by flukes a year! Check! They suck on their hosts making them nutrient deficient! Check! The eight ways that lung flukes affect you! Check! Why didn't any of my medical doctors pick up the possibility of parasites? Hmm... Wait, I did ask my OB/GYN to order a parasite stool sample, but of course, it was negative. Too bad they don't run the outlawed Darkfield (Live Blood Cell) Microscopy test.

It is funny how we all know that parasites exist in other countries, but for some reason, we think they need a VISA to get into our country, the USA. Check out what CDC has to say about parasites:

Several parasitic diseases occur occasionally in the United States and more frequently in developing countries, but their

---

[37] "NEWSLETTER." *Pinnacle Health Wellness Catalog*. Web. <http://www.wellness24.org/fluke-parasites-the-intestinal-human-parasite-a-61.html>

prevalence has not been well studied. They include strongyloidiasis, caused by a worm infection that is of particular danger for children with an impaired immune system. It is acquired when larvae (immature worms) in soil contaminated with infected human feces come into contact with and penetrate the skin. They also include visceral toxocariasis, spread when children ingest soil contaminated with dog or cat feces containing the eggs of cat or dog roundworms, and cutaneous larva migrans, transmitted when children walk barefoot on soil contaminated with cat or dog hookworm larvae that penetrate their skin.

Other parasitic diseases are rare among children in the United States, but are widespread and account for a major disease burden among children in developing countries. The most important of these is malaria. Children in malaria-endemic countries are at high risk of the ill effects of malaria infection. The majority of the world's malaria deaths are in African children under 5 years of age.

Children in the United States are also at high risk for malaria infection when traveling to a malaria-endemic country. Children should be sure to take antimalarial drugs before, during, and after the trip, use repellant, sleep under an insecticide-treated bed net or in an air-conditioned room, and wear protective clothing.[38]

I think it is time for the CDC to update their information, which I doubt they will do because they don't want people to know what they really have. Years ago, medical doctors used to give kids medicine to help them get rid of parasites. It was a common practice.

---

38 "Children." *Centers for Disease Control and Prevention.* Centers for Disease Control and Prevention, 06 Oct. 2015. Web. <https://www.cdc.gov/parasites/children.html>

Everyone should do a parasite cleanse at least twice a year and stay on a maintenance program to help protect against new infestations. We de-parasite our pets and keep them on a preventative regime, why not us? Up until now, I have done them on and off for the last thirty years, thanks to Dr. Easterling and his mom's knowledge and acknowledgment of them.

With the rising awareness of these deadly parasites, I am now using PARATREX and LATERO-FLORA, by Dr. Edward Group III, DC, NP, DACBN, DCBCN, DABFM, parasite cleanse and maintenance program. PARATREX contains a Proprietary Blend of: Wildcrafted Black Walnut (green hull), Wildcrafted Epazote (leaf), Wildcrafted Neem (leaf), Organic Clove (bud), Organic Wormwood [Artemisia absinthium] (leaf/stem), Protease with DPPIV, Amylase, Glucoamylase, Lactase, Cellulase [I,II], Maltase, Hemicellulase, Xylanase, Beta Glucanase, Serrapeptase, Nattokinase, Bromelain, Papain, alpha Galactosidase, Lipase, Catalase, Invertase, Pectinase, Phytase, Glucose Oxidase. LATERO-FLORA contains Bacillus laterosporus (B.O.D. strain). Learn more about this cleanse kit at: www.globalhealingcenter.com/harmful-organism-cleansing-kit.html

My "Mental" Intervention

When I got home from the Born Clinic, my husband had, unannounced to me, arranged for an intervention on me with my sons. Our boys had come home from college for Labor Day weekend. As soon as I walked in the door my husband asked me to sit down in the living room so we could all talk. Unfortunately, I had to throw up.

When I finished throwing up, I slowly made it downstairs for my "intervention." Sitting and listening to each one's concerns about me not eating and throwing up, I informed them that, "This is why I went to the Born Clinic today! To get help and to hopefully be able to stop throwing up!"

My husband then said, "You don't have Lyme disease since the Western blot test came back negative." I reminded him of all the calls from my doctor's office in the last six days, informing me that even if the Western blot came back positive, it wasn't accurate and I needed the IGeneX test done. He then said, "Your test was negative and the doctors said you don't have Lyme disease! The doctors at the Born Clinic are not real doctors!"

I told him, "Yes they are!" I then went on to inform all of them about the Zyto machine and what it picked up and that I was going back on Tuesday for more IV nutrition and to get the IGeneX test done!

My husband was furious! He told me, "No, you are not getting the IGeneX test because we have no money for that 'kind of care' since both boys are now in college." I was shocked! Really, here we own a successful heating and cooling company and he had told me early that month that we were probably going to receive a huge bonus in January! I thought that would be enough to cover whatever treatments I needed. Unfortunately, he didn't think I needed the treatments and that they were a waste of money.

This is why I am so grateful for direct sales and the financial freedom it has given me. Even though I was unable to work at this time, I had incredible credit. All of our household credit cards were in my name, including the credit cards I use for my business.

My husband told me, in front of our sons, that if I went ahead with treatments, they wouldn't be able to go to college! Horrified he was even saying this in front of them, I finally said, "Well, they will have to go to a community college until I am better to help pay for their college then!" This did not make my husband happy, I assure you.

Finally, I just flat out said, "I have my own credit cards, and I will use them to get help! You cannot tell me what to do!" He then said, "You need to go to your follow-up appointment with your regular medical doctor on Wednesday, and tell her that you still think you have Lyme disease." I agreed and went back upstairs to be alone.

One by one, my boys came up to check on me and to see if I was okay! It meant the world to me, to know that they still cared and loved me! Of course, as a mom, I didn't want to hold them back from getting their college degrees. I loved them so much and would have moved Heaven and Earth if I could have.

FACT: Doctors are not gods! They don't know everything, and when they misdiagnose their patients, they ruin families. If you are suffering and don't have much support, keep fighting and don't give up! If I can survive, you can too!

How to Stop Throwing Up

Dr. Easterling told me to eat white rice and homemade, sugar-free applesauce. "This is the ONLY time ever, one should eat white rice," he said. So, my son, Matt, made me some white rice and applesauce that night. That was the last time I threw up! In the morning I had a little bit more white rice and applesauce before I started my deep tissue cleanse. Praise God! Not being able to eat or keep liquids down is not any fun, I assure you.

Don't Let Other People's Belief Systems Stop You from Getting Better

On Tuesday, September 5th, my friend Kim Ellicott drove me to the Born Clinic for my IGeneX test, IV Nutrition plus more Zyto. Kim is a true friend! Even though she doesn't do a lot of supplements for herself, only a "natural" diet, she definitely believes in holistic medicine based on what she had witnessed with me. This is a sign of a true friend; they stand by your side, no matter what their belief system is!

When my husband got home on Tuesday, he was angry that I had gone to get the IGeneX test done. He then told me that he was going with me to my regular Western medicine doctor appointment to tell her that I was crazy because I still thought I had Lyme disease. I told him, "No! You aren't going with me to my appointment. You haven't gone with me to see most of my specialists, and now you want to tell my doctor I am nuts! I don't think so!"

This happens often when a spouse has a chronic disease. The other spouse can't handle the stress or they feel helpless, so they give up on them. I understood this, so to get better, I brought this fact to mind, and I replaced my anger and bad thoughts with, "I am not a victim, and I know this is common human behavior. Therefore, I am not letting what my husband thinks influence my decision on how to heal."

I drove myself to my doctor's appointment the next morning. When I got there, my doctor was very worried about me. She told me that my husband had called and wanted her to call him regarding me. For the first time, I realized that I had to share my fears with her about my husband. After I shared in detail what he had been doing, she told me that he will never change and that I should leave him. This was an eye opener to me. I had been fighting to save my marriage for so long; I now realized that I had lost myself in the process. At the time, I didn't listen to her. I didn't want to give up on my marriage!

I ended up not telling my doctor about the IGeneX test for fear that she might call my husband and say I was crazy. I wanted to have the test back first, so I could show her. She took my blood pressure and wanted to give me heart meds and have me wear a heart monitor for a few days. I told her I would be okay; it was the white coat making my heart race. I had my blood pressure taken the day before at the Born Clinic, and it was fine. I wonder if this was because I was now feeding my thyroid and not destroying my health with the synthetic thyroid medications? According to the Mayo Clinic, "When the thyroid gland doesn't produce enough thyroid hormone (hypothyroidism) or produces too much thyroid hormone (hyperthyroidism), high blood pressure can result."[39]

I went back again on Friday for my third IV Nutrition. Once again, Jordan asked me about mold and living in Detroit. I said to him, "I do not live in Detroit, nor do I have a Michigan style basement."

On the way home, I got a text from a nurse friend who had talked with my husband. She was angry that I listened to the "crazies" at the Born Clinic and that I had decided to invest $500 in the IGeneX test, since my regular doctor's office told me that I did not have Lyme disease. She said that the doctors at the University of Michigan were highly trained. Why would I listen to a guy that uses

---

[39]   "Symptoms and Causes." *Mayo Clinic.* 09 Sept. 2016. <http://www.mayoclinic.org/diseas-es-conditions/secondary-hypertension/symptoms-causes/dxc-20184438>

a Zyto machine? I was horrified thinking that my husband was able to influence some of my most trusted family members and friends by telling them I was crazy for still thinking I had Lyme disease.

I now know that it wasn't just because of his belief. If you search the web, you will see that it is still being taught in medical school that Lyme disease is rare and that Chronic Lyme Disease does NOT exist! Yale University owns the patent on the fake/failed LYMErix Vaccine and the Test Kits, along with everyone they are in bed with, which makes it hard to find the truth when searching the web about Lyme disease.[40] I will discuss this more in Chapter 10.

On Friday, September 5, 2014, (a week into my holistic treatment at the Born Clinic) my daughter Brittany intervened from Denver and had my husband stay somewhere else for a few days, leaving me home alone for the weekend. I didn't mind being left alone, I was just sad that here I was fighting for my life, and my husband, certain family members and friends didn't believe I was really sick.

I can totally relate to Yolanda Forster from the reality TV show, "Real Housewives of Beverly Hills." Yolanda has Lyme disease. Other housewives on the show were saying she wasn't really sick, but instead had Münchausen syndrome. According to WebMD, "Münchausen syndrome is a factitious disorder, a mental disorder in which a person repeatedly and deliberately acts as if he or she has a physical or mental illness when he or she is not really sick. Münchausen syndrome is considered a mental illness because it is associated with severe emotional difficulties."[41]

Associated with severe emotional difficulties? Of course, all

---

[40]   "TruthCures." *Vimeo*. Web. <https://vimeo.com/truthcures>

[41]   "Mental Health: Munchausen Syndrome." *WebMD*. WebMD. Web. <http://www.webmd.com/mental-health/munchausen-syndrome>

Lyme patients have this as part of their list of illnesses, because every single one of us Lyme patients goes through emotional difficulties imposed by the "Powers that Be" not recognizing this disease.

Since Lyme is not acknowledged, we all must be crazy! Here is a fine example of a "Get out of Jail Free" card for medical doctors. If you can't give it a name/diagnoses, it must be mental.

It is an outrage that Lyme disease is not recognized as a serious and life threatening disease. Instead, everyone thinks you are crazy or depressed. This is what makes Lyme disease the new scarlet letter.

Don't despair! Go to my *Life Healing Handbook* at
www.OvercomingLymeDisease.com/free-handbook
to learn more about daily tips to have
a healthier life, recipes, and more.

PART TWO

Healing From the Inside Out

CHAPTER 5

Deep Tissue Cleanse: The Secret to Recovery

"There are seldom, if ever, any hopeless situations, but there are many people who lose hope in face of some situations."
–Zig Ziglar

My friend Kim Ellicott and my brother Richie came over the next day. They were shocked that I had to drive myself to the Born Clinic. My husband promised them that he would drive me to my appointment at the Born Clinic, but got mad at me for throwing up and left for work. On top of that, everything they had cleaned and worked on at the house two days prior was now a mess. Gotta love college kids!

Richie helped clean things up while Kim started making me what I needed for my deep tissue cleanse. She made potassium broth, Oat Straw, Flax and Chamomile Tea combination, and juiced organic carrots and apples for me to drink. She then boiled the herbs for my herbal colemas and made some organic coffee for my coffee enemas. All of this I had learned thirty years ago from my mentor and nutritionist, Virginia Easterling Jenkins.

An herbal colema is like a high colonic. They both use five gallons of purified warm water, but an herbal colema uses herbs that heal the gut. A colema flushes out your colon as it removes fecal matter that has been stuck to the colon wall, along with other toxins, parasites, poisons, or waste material. The problem with high colonics is that they do not have any healing herbs in them, and if the person giving you the colonic allows the water to enter in your colon under too much pressure or if the water is too hot or cold, it can cause more harm than good.

Doing a 7-day deep tissue cleanse was the game changer for me. Of course, I was already on the supplements I needed for my body: Lauricidin, Vera-Thera CF, Cytozyme-THY, Colloidal Silver, the special brand of enzymes, and the Endo-met supplements from my HTMA. The 7-day deep tissue cleanse cleaned out toxins from my colon, so the endotoxins from the mold and Lyme could not get reabsorbed in my intestines. It helped remove heavy metals, damage from medications, and helped remove parasites and worms from my colon. In turn, it helped clean the toxic overload in my bad cells which allowed new, healthy cells to grow. In other words, it helped with the methylation cycle in my cells.

During this time, I started to realize that I needed to treat Lyme like cancer. I needed to focus on the Gerson Therapy, one of the best therapies out there for cancer or any disease. The Gerson Therapy calls for juice fasting and coffee enemas.[42] I had learned about the Gerson Therapy years ago from Virginia and Rich. They used it to help treat their cancer patients and had great success when their patients followed the protocol they suggested. Rich would always

---

[42] "The Gerson Therapy." *Gerson Institute*. 20 Oct. 2016. Web.
<http://gerson.org/gerpress/the-gerson-therapy/>

say that if he could keep his cancer patients from eating foods they shouldn't, they would stay well.

In the book *Mum's Not Having Chemo*, Laura Bond touches on a great cancer treatment called Hyperthermia:

> 'Hyperthermia helps the immune system to recognise and destroy tumour cells,' says Dr. Jacob. Dr. Alexander Herzog, head of Dr. Herzog's Special Hospital near Frankfurt explains the process in more detail: 'The treatment helps to develop heat shock proteins on the surface of the tumour cells, making them more visible to the attack of the immune system.'

Later, Laura shares in her book:

> Detoxification is important before embarking on hyperthermia, according to the experts: 'Free radicals will sidetrack the immune system for the real challenge,' says Dr. Trefzer, who believe treatments are more effective if the patient has done some sweating, exercise and fasting beforehand.[43]

This is HUGE! Detoxification and cleaning out your gut, via a fast, are the most important things you can do for your immune system! This is why I healed faster than most people and why my treatments worked better. I had done a Deep Tissue Cleanse and continued to work on my gut via following the Gerson Therapy. Deep Tissue Cleanse goes a little deeper and helps heal the colon faster.

---

[43] Bond, Laura. *Mum's NOT Having Chemo: Cutting-edge Therapies, Real-life Stories - a Road-map to Healing from Cancer*. London: Piatkus, 2013. Print.

My Past Positive Experiences in Healing the Body

I started seeing Virginia Easterling Jenkins for nutritional guidance during my freshman year of college. Like most of us do when we go away to college, I ate poorly and gained weight.

Via a hair analysis, iridology and her wise intuition, Virginia put me on supplements and a diet for my body. For the first time in my life, my bowels started to move on a regular, daily basis and my periods became normal. Every time Virginia did a hair analysis on me, she would ask if I had had a recent infection or if I was just getting over one. Dr. Easterling would question me too at times.

Of course, my health issues improved. However, once we start feeling better, most of us revert back to our old habits of bad eating.

This is why it is important to be accountable to someone, via a friend, mentor, lifestyle coach, or a positive knowledgeable support group. More now than ever, people are hiring personal lifestyle coaches to help them stay on course with their treatments. It is hard to stay on track with your healing when your symptoms start to subside. When this happens, it is very natural to revert back to our old ways of living that aided in us getting sick in the first place. To form good, life-changing habits, hire a life or health coach.

3-Day Deep Tissue Cleanse

My beautiful daughter, Brittany, was born in May, 1988. What was supposed to be an easy hospital birth ended up becoming a nightmare! Brittany was two weeks late and breach. Fortunately, Brittany did flip back to face downward the night before I was going in to have a C-section. Instead, I was induced.

I had gone to a Lamaze class and was hoping for a drug-free labor. Instead, I ended up with an epidural after nine hours of heavy/painful labor. This is when things went downhill. As soon as the anesthesiologist gave me my epidural and left me alone on my side in the delivery room, I started to projectile vomit. It was thick, green vomit, and I could not stop it from going all over the baby monitor equipment next to me. It was totally disgusting; it reminded me of the girl in *The Exorcist*! It was that gross and uncontrollable.

When the nurse came in, she panicked and ran to me, placing a bowl in front of my mouth so I could finish throwing up in it, and wiped off my face in horror. I was told I had an allergic reaction to the injection. Or, was the needle contaminated? Years later, a family nurse anesthetist informed me that it must have gone in wrong and that they could have reversed it and done another one.

I ended up with a migraine for two weeks accompanied by postpartum depression. So, I sought the expert health advice of Virginia Easterling. Virginia put me on a 3-day deep tissue cleanse, which calls for herbal colemas, potassium broth, fresh organic carrot and golden delicious apple juice, flaxseed tea, and supplements that I needed for my body. It was a fast way to rid my body of the drug residue from the epidural and whatever other toxic things that were causing me to be ill. During my first colema, I became pain-free and my mental health improved. It is crucial that we take care of our gut health if we are going to get better.

Since I still didn't understand the dangers of vaccines, I had my precious daughter vaccinated. Each time, she ended up sick, and a few times, she had to be hospitalized with high fevers, ear infections, and breathing problems after receiving her vaccines. This is the so-called "normal and acceptable" side effect to vaccines, preached by their makers and everyone in bed with them.[44]

Virginia did a hair analysis on Brittany and told me that she had an egg allergy. Virginia said that was why she was getting sick. My precious daughter was getting the very virus that we were trying to protect her from. Regardless, I still wasn't convinced and I still had her vaccinated until age six. To see the toxic poisons they are injecting into humans, check out CDC vaccine ingredient list.[45]

By the way, I ended up having my last two children, Matt and Teddy, born at home with a Nurse Midwife named Pat Kramer. She was amazing! Unfortunately, I ended up vaccinating my son Matt up until he was two years of age. Up until then, I was still brainwashed that if you didn't vaccinate your children, you could kill them or cause them to be ill. I am happy to announce that my youngest son Teddy has never been vaccinated, and he was my healthiest child and still is.

Did you know, in the Middle Ages, midwives would not only assist in home births, but they would also be called upon to take care of the sick? They used herbs and other folk remedies for treatments. They were suspected of witchcraft and sorcery because some babies died during birth or were deformed. So, they were persecuted, arrested and even killed by the "Powers that Be." Thank goodness, we are no longer in the Middle Ages and hospitals are starting to see the importance of a natural birth again, as most hospitals and insurance companies cover midwives now.[46]

---

[44] "Possible Side-effects from Vaccines." *Centers for Disease Control and Prevention.* Centers for Disease Control and Prevention, 02 Dec. 2016. Web. <https://www.cdc.gov/vaccines/vac-gen/side-effects.htm>

[45] https://www.cdc.gov/VACCINEs/pubs/pinkbook/downloads/appendices/B/excipient-table-2.pdf

[46] Singingtree, Daphne. *Birthsong Midwifery Workbook.* Eugene, OR: Eagletree, 2006. Print.

New Changes and New Challenges

My first marriage did not last long. My daughter and I ended up moving into an apartment in Milan, Michigan. I worked two waitressing jobs and cleaned houses, to make ends meet.

One night, after a long waitressing shift at Weber's Inn, I tripped over a box that was left in the aisle. I fell hard, and my right inner arm and my armpit hooked the metal glass cleaner machine. I was in instant pain! We filed a workman's comp claim, and I went home on Ibuprofen. I tried resting, but the pain continued to get worse. So, I went to an Urgent Care. I had x-rays that showed my ribs were out of place, vertebrae twisted in my neck and mid-back, and I was bruised to the bone on my arm. They gave me some pain pills and sent me home.

The pain continued to get worse. I went back to the Urgent Care, and they gave me a muscle relaxer since my ribs were out. Still, no relief! By the third day, I could barely move, and it hurt each time I took a breath.

Long story short, I ended up seeing a pain specialist at St. Joseph Hospital. Via an MRI, I was diagnosed with nerve damage and was told that it would never heal because of the nerve being pinched. The ligaments and muscles in my ribs were pulled from the sternum. I had twisted vertebrae in my neck and upper back, along with major pain in my right arm from being bruised to the bone, nerve damage, and a sprung rotor cup. Workmen's comp diagnosed me with the same issues as the pain doctor, after torturing me with electrodes and a needle to see if there was nerve damage.

At first, they agreed with my pain doctor. Unfortunately, later they fought the case. Their doctor gave me twelve steroid shots in the back of my neck and shoulder. OUCH! I was in so much pain from the shots that I couldn't even pull off my pants when I went the bathroom for three days afterward! The doctors then put me in physical therapy, to no avail; I got even worse! Since then, I have learned that steroids are not good for people with Lyme disease because it can weaken your immune system and your bones.[47] [48]

I contacted my loving, caring, Christian cousin and chiropractor, Bill Thatcher. He worked on me three times a week to get my ribs and vertebrae back in place. As good as he was, the adjustments didn't stay and my pain continued. More than likely I had a fractured rib that no x-ray picked up.

A great tip I learned from my cousin is to read a chapter a day from The Book of Proverbs. In *The Holy Bible*, The Book of Proverbs has thirty-one chapters. A good system to stay connected to God's love for us and to grow in wisdom is to take a few minutes first thing in the morning and read a chapter a day. It really helps remind me of God's love and to trust Him during the storms of life. To this day, I still use this tip when I feel alone and need His wisdom and guidance.

4-Day Deep Tissue Cleanse

My pain doctor had me go in and get a shot in the middle of my throat/chest with a very long needle to deaden the nerve in my chest that was causing me pain. The shot did not work.

---

[47]   "Risks." *Mayo Clinic*. 02 July 2016. Web.
      <http://www.mayoclinic.org/tests-procedures/cortisone-shots/details/risks/cmc-20206857>

[48]   "Cortisone Injection (Corticosteroid Injection)." *WebMD*. WebMD. Web.
      <http://www.webmd.com/arthritis/what-are-cortisone-shots>

One day six months post-fall, after stopping to pick up some vitamins at the J-Rich Clinic, Virginia asked me, "Are you done yet?"

I asked her, "What are you talking about?"

She replied, "Are you done being tortured? If so, let's get you healed!"

Virginia started me on a 4-day Deep Tissue Cleanse. Within the first day, after my morning herbal colema, I was out of pain for the first time in months! My 4-day cleanse consisted of juicing organic veggies and fruit, herbal teas, potassium broth, eight glasses a day of purified water, supplements for my body, and an evening Bentonite Clay colema on the third night.

Bentonite Clay is great at absorbing toxins, pathogenic viruses, pesticides, and herbicides. Most people use Bentonite orally. The smartest way to do it is rectally, via a colema. The faster you can get these toxins out of you, the sooner you are going to feel better. Our colon is responsible for 70% of our immune system. With that being said, why are we so embarrassed to talk about our bowel movements or lack of? It is almost taboo to talk about going number two. Well, we need to change our ways in order to become healthy and create a healthy gut ecosystem.

After the 4-day deep tissue cleanse, Virginia started me on an organic diet filled with lightly steamed veggies, and free of gluten, dairy and sugar. You need to do a lightly steamed vegetable diet with fruit for a couple of days after coming off a deep tissue cleanse. If you go to steak and potatoes, you will shock your system. She also gave me aromatherapy massages, with rose hips and lavender oil. According to Dr. Mercola, "Lavender oil is known for its anti-inflammatory, antifungal, antidepressant, antiseptic, antibacterial and antimicrobial properties. It also has antispasmodic, analgesic, detoxifying, hypotensive and sedative effects. Lavender oil is one of the most well-known essential oils in aromatherapy."[49] Rosehips also provide great benefits by reducing inflammation:

> According to the University of Maryland, rosehip tea is a great option to help reduce inflammation in the body. Anyone suffering from osteoarthritis can benefit by having a cup of rosehip tea on a regular basis. *Arthritis Research UK* reported a study regarding the effects of rosehip for patients who had osteoarthritis. They found that those who were given rosehips had a positive affect versus those that were not.
>
> Ultimately, the rosehip significantly improved hip flexion when compared with the placebo. Significantly more participants in the active treatment group reported a reduction in pain compared with the placebo group. The rosehip group also had a reduction in some disease-related symptoms (like morning stiffness) and a significant decline in painkiller use. Reports have also shown that relief of inflammation be can be found by adding rosehip oil to your bath water. [50]

The reason why aromatherapy is so good for you is because your skin is your largest organ and is known as the third kidney. What you put on it matters because your skin absorbs whatever you put on it. Using God-given medicinal herbs and plants help your body heal faster, plus keeps you healthier by not adding more toxins to your body.

---

[49]   "Herbal Oil: Lavender Oil Benefits and Uses." *Mercola.com*. Web. <http://articles.mercola.com/herbal-oils/lavender-oil.aspx>

[50]   "Rosehip Oil: The Anti-Aging Oil?" *Dr. Axe*. Web. <https://draxe.com/rosehip-oil/>

Virginia had a special light, like what they have for Therma-Scans, to make sure the nerve in my chest was only being pinched and to rule out it being severed. Based on her findings, the nerve was only being pinched. Praise God!

Like I mentioned earlier, Rich and Karen are also close to a world-renowned chiropractor that helped start the International College of Applied Kinesiology, Dr. George Koffeman. Rich suggested that I go see Dr. Koffeman because he believed he could help me.

What is Applied Kinesiology?

Applied Kinesiology (AK) is a system of diagnostic and treatment protocols originated by Dr. George Goodheart, and further developed by other chiropractic physicians of the International College of Applied Kinesiology (ICAK), that enable the doctor of chiropractic to determine and effectively treat the underlying cause of the patient's symptoms by addressing metabolic imbalances and nutritional deficiencies, virtually the most common underlying cause of most human health issues.[51]

Sure enough, Dr. George Koffeman was amazing! I only had to go in twice the first week. My adjustments started to hold! I went weekly for six weeks, then every other week, to once a month! I now go whenever I feel pain or when my ribs go out of place.

Since I had little to no money to pay for my treatments, I helped Virginia out in her clinic, in exchange for her nutritional guidance and supplements, from 1991-1995.

---

[51] "Adobe Chiropractic - Chiropractor In Temecula, CA USA: Meet Dr. Rocco." *Adobe Chiropractic - Chiropractor In Temecula, CA USA: Meet Dr. Rocco.* Web. <http://www.doctorbennrocco.com/about-us.html>

Working with Virginia, I learned so much! I witnessed firsthand many miracles! One particular story that stands out to me was a nine-month old baby boy with eczema. This poor child stuck to his own crib sheets. His precious baby skin would rip off each time his loving parents would try to pick him up. Talk about heartbreak and agony, to see your baby suffer like that.

This southern family came hundreds of miles to seek treatment with Virginia, after consulting with numerous specialists, including the Mayo Clinic. Within a few days to a week, this poor child's skin started to heal, and he no longer stuck to his bedding. I can't remember everything this child was given, but a couple of things that I do recall are: rice bran syrup, liquid chlorophyll, and probiotics, along with garlic and probiotic enemas, via a sterile baby nose syringe, using warm distilled water. Virginia also placed him on an organic diet which was also gluten, dairy, and sugar-free. The parents would use a food processor or a hand grinder, which you can buy at most health food stores, to make fresh organic baby food. They also started using Real Purity skin care products. They are chemical free, instead of the standard toxic baby products on the market.

This is the same treatment I started using on my daughter and my sons when they were young and got sick. It is better than any hospital treatment or failed antibiotic program.

For more info on deep tissue cleansing, infant and
postpartum health, and Virginia's protocols,
check out my *Life Healing Handbook* at
www.OvercomingLymeDisease.com/free-handbook.

CHAPTER 6

Seeing Beyond Your Disbelief

"Clutter is not just physical stuff. It's old ideas,
toxic relationships and bad habits. Clutter is anything that
does not support your better self."
–Eleanor Brown

The hardest thing to overcome is the loss of your health. You have to be willing to deal with your past so that those negative thoughts and emotions don't continue to influence your life and the cells in your body.

What Are You Focusing On?

"Our thoughts are things."
–Zig Ziglar

In Laura Bond's book *Mum's Not Having Chemo,* Dr. Kelly Turner, a New York–based cancer counselor, researcher, and author of *Radical Remission,* shared successful treatments and beliefs of cancer survivors:

After interviewing twenty subjects who defied a death sentence and talking to over fifty physicians and healers, Dr. Turner found common threads lines the path to recovery. The six most frequently mentioned treatments or beliefs were as follows:

1. Deepening one's spirituality
2. Trusting in intuition regarding health decisions
3. Releasing suppressed emotions
4. Feeling love/joy/happiness
5. Changing one's diet
6. Taking herbal or vitamin supplements.

Dr. Turner found this a common theme among her subjects: 'So many of the people I interviewed who have these amazing healings- they don't talk about killing their cancer- they talk about healing their cells and healing their immune systems,' she says.[52]

I love that! They talk about healing their cells and healing their immune systems, not about killing the cancer. That is exactly what I did, and it is what everyone with Lyme disease or any illness needs to focus on, healing and not killing your cells and your immune system.

Dr. Bernard Jensen, The Right Attitude

Virginia and Rich both studied and learned techniques taught by the late Bernard Jensen D.C., Nutritionist. Jensen was the owner and founder of the Hidden Valley Health Ranch, which served as a retreat for people all over the world to learn how to live a healthy

---

[52] Bond, Laura. *Mum's NOT Having Chemo: Cutting-edge Therapies, Real-life Stories - a Road-map to Healing from Cancer.* London: Piatkus, 2013. Print.

life.[53] They helped their patients do deep tissue cleanses, which helped heal them from all types of illnesses and diseases.

Bernard Jensen taught that not only is the condition of the bowel tissue often the key to the state of health or disease of an individual, but your mental attitude has a huge bearing as well.

In Jensen's book *Tissue Cleansing Through Bowel Management*, he talks about the Organic versus Functional:

> There are two conditions in people that I always take care of right away. It is difficult to separate these conditions and yet they represent two ways of treatment...People are dealing with both physical and mental imbalances and I get to the root of their problem by finding out what they believe in, what is at the bottom of their troubles...If you believe a lie, then you live a lie. If you believe in happiness, desire happiness and know how to go about attaining happiness, then chances are you are happy. However, the person who holds a vision of themselves as diseased, distressed, blue, trapped or unable to get well, has to be reeducated. They have created their own world and trapped themselves in it. Many are victims of percentage diagnoses— 'Your chances of getting well are only 30%,' and we have to erase this from their mind.
>
> We have an organic condition and a functional condition. When we deal with the organic condition we have to change the tissue, we have to change damaged cell structure, create a new chemical balance, promote better circulation; we have to remove obstructions, pressure and other gravitational effects.

---

[53] "Bernard Jensen." *Dr. Bernard Jensen | Holistic Healer, Iridology Leader.* Web. <http://www.bernardjensen.com/Bernard-Jensen_ep_43-1.html>

These things are strictly physical and we find that the mind alone cannot overcome them very well. I believe that the mind has a tremendous effect on the physical body but that we must feed each aspect its own kind of food. In the organic or physical aspect, we use diet, corrective exercise and tissue cleansing. We feed the mind or functional aspect of our being with education; teaching people to grow out of their problems, to change their attitude and consciousness. They must learn to walk the higher path in thoughts, words and deeds.[54]

Jensen goes on to say, "I have changed people's cell structure many times, actually showing them the results with blood tests, but they still hang onto their old attitudes. THEY WANT TO GET WELL BUT DON'T BELIEVE THEY CAN. THIS CONFUSED STATE IS TRANSFERRED TO EVERY CELL IN THE BODY. This is why I question people about their mental attitude; we have to see where we are before we know where to go."

Hering's Law of Cure

Dr. Jensen was a huge believer and follower of Hering's Law of Cure. It states that "All cures start from within out and from the head down and in reverse order as the symptoms have appeared."[55] I believe in this universal law, like the law of attraction or law of gravity. Our greatest healing power comes from within out. As we start to heal our bodies, mind, and spirit, past symptoms and/or

---

54   Jensen, Bernard, and Sylvia Bell. *Tissue Cleansing through Bowel Management: From the Simple to the Ultimate.* Summertown, TN: Book, 1981. Print.

55   "Hering's Law of Cure." *Healing Naturally by Bee.* Web. <https://www.healingnaturallybybee.com/herings-law-of-cure/>

emotions will pop up. We relive old symptoms because we need to go back through them to eradicate them. We need to realize this is a part of our healing process. In order to continue healing, we need to keep the course and not let these past symptoms or feelings that re-appear stop us along our journey to healing. We need to celebrate that the symptom comes up, sort of like peeling an onion, so we head back to the core of health.

To help you get better faster, I now believe you should find someone that is knowledgeable in NET, Mind-Body Stress Relief, to help you get unstuck from your past so your body can start the healing process. Dr. Horn used NET and kinesiology on me when I was having my infected root canals removed. I am now seeing her again for NET to further my healing process from all of the traumatic experiences from my past and it is awesome!

NET is based on the physiological foundations of stress-related responses. As discovered in the late 1970s, emotional responses are composed of neuropeptides (amino acid chains) and their receptors, which lie on neurons and other cells of remote tissues in the body. The neuropeptides are ejected from the neuron and carry the encoded "information" to other sites within the body. These neuropeptides are in a category of neurochemicals known as Information Substances (IS). ISs are released at times of stress-related arousal and become attached to remotely-positioned neuroreceptors.

Significantly, this process also happens when a person recalls to memory an event in which a stress originally occurred. This is a key factor in the NET treatment. Thus, the physiological status of the body is emotionally replicating a similar physiological state that was found in the original conditioning event by the process of remembering.[56]

The Carcinogenic Relationship

In Laura Bond's book *Mum's Not Having Chemo*, she talks about The Carcinogenic Relationship. She quotes one of the top holistic doctors of our time, the late leading cancer and Lyme specialist, Dr. Nicholas Gonzalez. From her book:

'A negative, hostile, angry spouse can undermine everything I do, because the patient lives in a state of fear and anxiety.' Early on in his career, Dr. Gonzalez realized that emotional health was just as important as the enzyme therapy and coffee enemas he was prescribing to patients. 'Nutrition is wonderful, but there is no vitamin, mineral or trace element that can override somebody's psychology,' he says. 'Under stress the body tissues break down to provide energy to deal with the stress – and that's the antithesis of healing.'

A prime example of the 'carcinogenic relationship' recently walked into Dr. Gonzalez's office. The patient, a woman with ovarian cancer, was keen to start work with Dr. Gonzalez, but her husband was clearly against it: 'He came into the room, arms folded, and within ten seconds he said, "How do I know we can trust you and that this isn't just a bunch of quackery?" and I said, "You know something? You can't know that." I then said to the patient: "You told me, your husband was supportive?" The

---

[56] "An Introduction to NET." *NETmindbody*. Web. <https://www.netmindbody.com/more-information/an-introduction-to-net>

husband left the room and his wife said to me, "He does it all the time." I didn't say this to her, but I could see right away that the main reason she had cancer was she was living with a bully.'[57]

What is holding you back from believing you can get better? Is it your spouse? Is it from the abuse you had suffered from as a child or as an adult? Is it something you did that you need to ask forgiveness for? Is it a feeling that you don't deserve to be better? Is it financial? No matter what it is, I am a firm believer that you can overcome it by renewing your mind and starting to love yourself and see yourself as God sees you.

Epigenetics

Laura Bond has a chapter in *Mum's Not Having Chemo* called "The Cancer Personality." In it, she writes:

> Ancient wisdom and common sense tell us that feelings of hopelessness, frustration and anxiety can destroy our immune systems and wreak havoc on our health. When tension headaches take hold or when our skin suddenly breaks out we'll shrug our shoulders and admit we're 'under a lot of pressure' or 'stressed to the max', but now science is giving credence to this intuitive connection; research from Stanford University Medical School reveals that 95 per cent of all illness is stress-related. And yet, when it comes to cancer, we can't shake the belief that stress is irrelevant and that smoking, bad genes and bad luck are the best predictors of the disease. Nothing

---

[57] Bond, Laura. *Mum's NOT Having Chemo: Cutting-edge Therapies, Real-life Stories - a Road-map to Healing from Cancer.* London: Piatkus, 2013. Print.

could be further from the truth; 'The genes don't make the decision,' says Dr. Bernie Siegel, cancer surgeon and best-selling author. 'They're stimulated by the internal chemistry, which is called epigenetics.'

The epigenome is located on top of the genome (hence the prefix 'epi', meaning above). We now know that environmental factors like diet and stress can switch genes on and off. 'We can't change our genes, but we can change their function and expression,' writes Dr. Mark Hyman in his book *The Blood Sugar Solution*. 'The collective experience of our lives--our intrauterine environment, diet, toxins, microbes, allergens, stresses, social connections, thoughts and beliefs -- control which genes are turned on and off.'

Genes do not control your destiny -- that's the take-home message from the exciting field of epigenetics: 'The vast majority of diseases we suffer from -- diabetes, obesity, heart disease, cancer -- are multifactorial lifestyle diseases,' says integrative health specialist Chris Kressor. 'Genetics may determine our predisposition to these conditions, but those genes must be activated (or silenced) by environmental triggers such as diet and stress in order to cause disease.'

In other words, your diet, mind, and belief system play huge roles in helping you get better.

In the book, Laura Bond also talks about the Type C Personality and how it relates to developing cancer.

The five characteristics are:
- Always putting others first
- Low self-esteem
- Bottling up emotions
- Living in fear
- Harbouring resentment[58]

The Dangers of Mold

My last IV nutrition and Zyto were done on Monday, September 8th. This time, Jordan only asked if I had a leak in my basement. I told him, "No, we have no leaks." When I got back to my house, my husband was home with a better attitude. I went upstairs and took a bath. When I got out, I told him about the Zyto picking up mold again. We went downstairs, and guess what we found? Water in our basement from a burst pipe.

We had some drywall installed earlier that year, and the workers put a nail in the water pipe to the outside faucet. When we turned on the inside valve to the outdoor faucet, our leak began. This was in May. By June, I was deathly ill and ended up in the ER and was diagnosed that time with hypothyroid.

It totally makes sense why my health deteriorated very quickly. We had mold in the house, and mold mixed with Lyme disease is NOT good! It makes the symptoms even worse because the Lyme spirochete sheds fungal antigens, also known as endotoxins. Mold acts the same way when you try to get rid of it; it produces endotoxins.

---

58 Bond, Laura. *Mum's NOT Having Chemo: Cutting-edge Therapies. Real-life Stories - a Road-map to Healing from Cancer.* London: Piatkus, 2013. Print.

According to National Treatment Centers for Environmental Disease:

> Endotoxins are toxins (poisons) that are released by gram-negative bacteria into the environment, which are toxins kept within the bacterial cell and are released only after destruction of the bacterial cell wall.

> The bacteria that produce endotoxins grow alongside fungus/mold in indoor water damaged environments. These gram-negative bacteria harbor in the human digestive tract and are a source of inflammation in the gut and in other parts of the body.

> Endotoxins have been documented to cause inflammation throughout the body, onset clinical diabetes, obesity, nausea, vomiting, diarrhea, fever, disseminated intravascular coagulation, vascular collapse, and organ failure.[59]

With Lyme disease, you also have biotoxins being released when you try to rid your body of it. According to Cure Zone:

> Endotoxins are a made of two parts: a fat or lipid bound to a polysaccharide chain in the lyme bug's outer shell. Endotoxins are like other biotoxins in that their goal is to help the bug survive. Some endotoxins are released in the body to make it safe for new lyme bugs, or when attacked by your immune system attack cells. The full actions and types of Lyme biotoxins and endotoxins is unknown.

---

[59] "Endotoxin, Endotoxins and Human Health." *National Treatment Centers for Environmental Disease.* Web.

Biotoxins exist in many types of creatures: tetanus, botulinum (botox), spiders, algae, ascaridin (gut parasites), staph, strept, babasia, lyme, special fish, chlamydia, tuberculosis, fungus or molds and viruses. Biotoxins are proposed to be tiny molecules used to survive by affecting the host's body in many ways that helps the infecting agent survive.[60]

Yes, those sound like the same symptoms as Lyme disease. Did you know when you contract Lyme disease this is what happens?

1. The spirochete gets into the lymphatic system within twenty-four hours
2. They stop your B cells from working which destroys your immune system
3. Borrelia synergies with dormant viruses like herpes and Epstein-Barr to wreck havoc on your immune system by causing immunosuppression and b cell dysfunction.

In other words, it causes immunosuppression. When mixed with any dormant virus in your body, it causes Post-Sepsis Syndrome or chronic neurological Lyme disease.

The Importance of Daily Coffee Enemas

From the book *Mum's Not Having Chemo* by Laura Bond:

Book into any holistic health retreat today and you're likely to find colonics or enemas on the itinerary. But it might surprise you to know that enemas are actually as conventional as they come.

---

[60] "Lyme Endotoxins/Biotoxins and Leptin at Rife Forum: Bio Resonance, Topic 1559704." *CureZone.org: Educating Instead of Medicating.* Web.

'Every hospital was once equipped with colon hydrotherapy machines or enemas,' says Matt Monarch a US-based raw-food guru. 'They were pretty much the first measure any nurse or doctor ever utilized when helping someone heal.' ...

While some might dismiss coffee enemas as a hippy fad, they were actually included in the Merck Manual — considered the conventional medical Bible — right up until 1977. 'When I spoke to the editor, he said the only reason they took them out was because they thought it was a little "folksy",' says Dr. Gonzalez. 'They wanted to put more high-tech stuff in.'

Although coffee enemas might be written off as quackery, conventional medical literature is littered with research supporting their benefits. For over a century, coffee enemas have been used to treat a wide range of illnesses, from migraines and eczema to septic shock and psychological disorders. 'I have a paper from 1922, published in the New England Journal of Medicine, which describes how a group at Harvard Medical School successfully treated what we call today "bipolar", with enemas,' says Gonzalez. "They got them off drugs and out of the hospital."[61]

Coffee enemas are like a blood transfusion. They help rid your body of the biotoxins so they aren't reabsorbed into the bloodstream via the colon. Every three minutes, all of the blood in our body is filtered through the liver. The liver dumps the toxins into our bowels. The longer we wait to go the bathroom, the more chance these toxins will continue to circulate in our body, making us ill.

---

[61] Bond, Laura. *Mum's NOT Having Chemo: Cutting-edge Therapies. Real-life Stories - a Road-map to Healing from Cancer*. London: Piatkus, 2013. Print.

Nowadays, hospitals use synthetic and extremely dangerous new drugs that can destroy your beneficial bacteria and can disturb the mechanism of elimination. It can take weeks or months for this mechanism to restart. Deep tissue cleansing and coffee enemas are great to clean these toxins out and to get the colon working properly again.

Knowing all of this, can you see why I feel the Zyto does pick up the frequencies of these things that are going on in our body? Of course, you need a knowledgeable tech to read it. Jordan is one of the best. Jordan even helped program the machine, so he knows what he is talking about.

Unfortunately, holistic doctors can't claim that it is accurate, unless they want to lose their license or be sued! The FDA won't allow the Zyto to be a part of helping with diagnostic testing. There isn't any so-called "scientific proof," it works. Then again, running a blood test doesn't always pick up the disease either and there are plenty of chances for human error. Most doctors just sign off on whatever the lab says, which is crazy since the lab tech does not know the patient and their symptoms.

While the medical world can be incredibly frustrating, remember that there is a lot that you can do at home to help cleanse your body and improve your overall health. For more information about deep tissue cleansing, coffee enemas and more, go to my *Life Healing Handbook* at **www.OvercomingLymeDisease.com/free-handbook**.

CHAPTER 7

Oxygen Therapies
and Miracle Medicine

*"We still don't know one thousandth of one percent
of what nature has revealed to us."*
–Albert Einstein

I ended up doing only four IV nutrition treatments at the Born Clinic because they don't use hydrogen peroxide to treat Lyme disease. Dr. Easterling worked with Dr. Jill Warner in Tennessee for many years. Together, they successfully treated Lyme patients with IV hydrogen peroxide (H2O2) instead of antibiotics, along with a personalized protocol for their body, which included enzymes. So, to get better, Rich wanted me to find a doctor in Michigan that used H2O2.

LEARNING TIP FOR DOCTORS: If you want to help your patients heal, partner with an ND, DO, or chiropractor who knows about enzymes and nutrition.

How I Found Dr. David Nebbeling

On Monday, September 8th, I found three doctors in Michigan from the free online book called *The Truth About Food Grade Hydrogen Peroxide*. You can find the free e-book on my website www. OvercomingLymeDisease.com.

I called the closest doctor on the list, which was Dr. David Nebbeling, a DO. He had a last-minute opening and was able to get me in two days later.

Ultraviolet Blood Irradiation (UVBI)

Dr. Nebbeling did a full exam on me and went over all my medical records. Dr. Nebbeling was concerned about my root canals being infected and encouraged me to get my mercury fillings removed. He then started me on photoluminescence (UVBI) treatments that day to help with any infections, including bone infection, that I may have been experiencing.

While waiting for my treatment to be done, I noticed a book for sale in their office called *Learn How the Top 20 Alternative Doctors in America Can Improve Your Health*, by Dr. Edward Kondrot. Of course, it interested me, so I bought it. Guess who was in it? Dr. David Nebbeling. In the book, Dr. Nebbeling explains the benefits of UVBI or Ultraviolet Blood Irradiation:

> We're actually able to treat any viruses or infections in the blood. It's very good for people who have chronic fatigue syndrome or multiple mixed bacterial infections, and even people with unhealed bone infections. It is an oxidative therapy for the blood.

It has wonderful benefits in balancing our nervous system and stimulating the immune system, as well as deactivating toxins and helping us fight bacterial infections and viruses in our body. It has wonderful applications for many things, from hepatitis C infections, to MRSA infections, but also for chronic fatigue syndrome, people with asthma, and some autoimmune diseases such as rheumatoid arthritis.[62]

Interesting how UVBI helps people diagnosed with rheumatoid arthritis. Rheumatoid arthritis is usually Lyme disease, and people that have gone on an antibiotic for something else usually discover that their joints don't ache as much. This has a lot to do with the spirochete changing its form and moving on to other areas in the body to take over and destroy.

UVBI, Ultraviolet Light Blood Irrigation, is a treatment where they take a big vial of blood out of your arm and inject it into a bag of saline solution, followed by a shot of ozone into the solution:

Ozone is an oxygen allotrope, O3, created by solar UV radiation and lightning. It's the strongest naturally occurring oxidant. Scripps Institute reported that ozone is actually generated by immune cells (Bablor, et. al., 2003) as part of its armamentarium of oxidants, which can be hurled against pathogens. Other immune system generated anti-infection oxidants include singlet oxygen, H2O2, NO, and NaOCl.[63]

Via an IV, they run the blood solution through a UV light before it re-enters your body. This procedure helps neutralize the

---

[62] Kondrot, Edward, and Abram Ber. *Learn How the Top 20 Alternative Doctors in America Can Improve Your Health*. Charleston, SC: Advantage, Member of Advantage Media Group, 2014. Print.

[63] "Ebola Cured With Ozone." Robert Rowen, MD and Teresa Su, MD. Web.

biotoxins and endotoxins in your blood that come from the die-off of Lyme, mold, co-infections, or whatever created the toxins that wreak havoc on your body. Antibiotics only kill bacteria; they do not neutralize the parasitic spirochete fungal antigens being shed into your lymphatic system that eventually shut down your B cells, causing post-sepsis. If you don't neutralize this biotoxin or endotoxin, your cells will stay toxic and new cells being formed will too. This is why oxygen therapies are important in restoring your health.

Meet Dr. David Steenblock, a Leading Stem Cell Expert

As mentioned earlier, I had numerous cancer scares and was highly concerned, based on my bone scan, that I may have lymphoma. I had done some research that showed how the "bacteria" that causes Lyme can develop into lymphoma. With the recurring fractured rib and the four huge calcified lymph nodes on my sternum, it may have gone into my bones, which is where your new B cells are made.[64]

In the book *Learn How the Top 20 Alternative Doctors in America Can Improve Your Health*, I read about Dr. David Steenblock, a leading stem cell expert:

> Dr. David Steenblock is one of the leading world authorities on stem cell therapy of all types having treated over 5,000 patients with bone marrow transplants, fat stem cells, or umbilical cord stem cells. Dr. Steenblock was trained as a biochemist, a pathologist, a surgeon, a physician, and research scientist and

---

64   Borrelia Infection and Risk of Non-Hodgkin Lymphoma." *Borrelia Infection and Risk of Non-Hodgkin Lymphoma | Blood Journal.* Web.
<http://www.bloodjournal.org/content/111/12/5524?sso-checked=true>

has taken care of 50,000 patients over the past 43 years. For the last ten years, he has specialized in the use of stem cells to treat a great variety of medical and health problems that otherwise were untreatable and incurable. Stem cells are a very hot topic for anyone who has any kind of chronic health problem since the results have been phenomenal for a great variety of different difficult-to-treat medical problems.

Dr. Steenblock goes on to say:

> I have developed a wide range of different techniques for treating people with difficult-to-treat problems. We use the hyperbaric oxygen, external counter pulsation (ECP), pulsed electromagnetic field therapy, chelation therapy, periodic acceleration, intravenous therapies, hyperthermia, intermittent hypoxia, bone marrow, fat, and other stem cell treatments, platelet-rich plasma treatments, and nutritional therapies.
>
> We've gone from hyperbaric oxygen in the late 1980's for patients with stroke and traumatic injury to the use of stem cells. We've developed some new techniques on this procedure, and we're getting great results. I have many testimonials on www.youtube.com (type in "Dr. Steenblock") and www.stemgevity.com.[65]

Dr. Steenblock is also the author of the first book for the public on the clinical use of umbilical cord-derived stem cell therapies. I recommend *Umbilical Cord Stem Cell Therapy* to anyone who wants a good understanding of stem cells.

---

65   Kondrot, Edward, and Abram Ber. *Learn How the Top 20 Alternative Doctors in America Can Improve Your Health*. Charleston, SC: Advantage, Member of Advantage Media Group, 2014. Print.

Stemgevity

Dr. Steenblock is "the creator of a stem cell–enhancing product called Stemgevity, which increases the number of stem cells in your blood stream while also increasing the stem cell's strength." Being my own doctor and advocate, I called and ordered some Stemgevity and started to take it. I was going to spare no expense in getting better. According to the Stemgevity site, "Stemgevity is a unique formulation of natural, synergistic herbs, vitamins, minerals, and plant extracts that many consider to be helpful for the support of the normal structure and function of your body's stem cells."[66]

Dr. Steenblock has used bone marrow stem cells to help treat lots of diseases and conditions. Here are just a few: ALS [Lou Gehrig's, Amyotrophic Lateral Sclerosis], Alzheimer's, anemia, lupus, systemic lupus erythematosus, severe lupus, lymphoma, non-Hodgkin's, metabolic syndrome, and multiple sclerosis. Go to his Stemgevity website to see more.

I used Stemgevity before bed to help me sleep and to help strengthen and increase my stem cells. It has 12 mg of a natural form of lithium in it, called lithium aspartate, which helps you rest better by calming your nerves.

Why Bioidentical Hormones?

I went back every other day for the following two weeks to get UVBI Treatments. It was during this time that Dr. Nebbeling reviewed my blood work and ordered my Bioidentical Hormones from O'Brien Pharmacy. The hormones are in the form of a troche,

---

66 "Stem Cell Mobilizing Formula Stemgevity." *Stemgevity*. Web. <http://stemgevity.com/>

a small lozenge that you put between your upper gums and lip to dissolve slowly. This is a safer way of taking your hormones because it gets right into the body and doesn't have to pass through your liver first.

Dr. David Nebbeling just completed his new and soon-to-be released book, *Breaking Grounds on Broken Bones*. In it, he shares the difference between bioidentical hormones and synthetic. Dr. Nebbeling also shares that:

> ...a properly balanced hormone program will treat and prevent osteopenia and osteoporosis, along with preventing insomnia, anxiety and depression, and dementia, it is important to stay on bioidentical hormones indefinitely. In addition to the above mentioned benefits, bioidentical hormones are truly an anti-cancer and anti-aging program. Patients should be looking foreword to getting on a balanced bioidentical hormone program and staying on it the rest of their lives! There is no need to fear hormones.

Dr. Nebbeling goes on to share the history of hormones:

> Is it safe to take hormones?

> Is it worth the risk to do hormone replacement therapy (HRT), or is hormone replacement therapy too risky to consider? And, how do the risks compare between HRT and bioidentical hormones?

> To answer this question, let's look at the history of the development of synthetic hormones. The pharmaceutical industry began their synthetic hormone product line with estrogen in the 1930s. Its promotion to and experimentation on

the American public began soon after. The synthetic estrogen DES was given to pregnant women between 1940 and 1971. It was prescribed to prevent miscarriage, premature labor, and related complications of pregnancy, and promote wellbeing. It claimed to 'make a normal pregnancy more normal.' DES was the first hormone product to be named as a human carcinogen.

In the 1960s, physicians were taught to give estrogen to postmenopausal women. The pharmaceutical companies promoted estrogen therapy to the American public as 'forever young, forever estrogen.' Estrogen became one of the top five prescription medications in America.

In 1975, estrogen was shown to cause cancer of the uterus. Shortly thereafter, the pharmaceutical industry's answer to this problem was to give synthetic progesterone with the estrogen. The variety of substances were called progestins. In July of 2002, after the Women's Health Initiative study had begun, there was a clearly established link between estrogen and progesterone hormone replacement therapy, and an increased risk for breast cancer. This was mentioned in all of the media. Perhaps the report of this study is what stays in the minds of many women today and adds to some of the confusion about hormone therapy.

When talking about hormone therapy, we have to consider the form of the hormone being given. Is it bioidentical or synthetic? We have to consider the method of its delivery, the amount being given, and the way it is being monitored.

Premarin®, though it comes from horses, is a mixture of 20 different types of estrogen in combination, and is delivered orally. The product goes to the digestive tract. It goes through the liver first, which is a significant stress on the body, and causes significant changes to the body, including an increase in blood clotting, and changes in cholesterol and metabolism. It increases and has been associated with risk of breast cancer and liver cancer. It is not surprising that women have hesitation about taking hormones for their bones. But synthetic hormones are only one part of the picture.[67]

It makes sense that I got so sick from the estrogen patch and when I tried the pill form. Notice synthetic hormones change your metabolism and are carcinogenic.

IGeneX Test Comes Back Positive

On September 30, 2014, my IGeneX test finally came back, and I was CDC IgM positive. CDC only recognizes that you may have Lyme disease if you have first tested positive on the ELISA test, showing an antibody response, and if you test positive on the Western blot test for five out of these ten IgG bands: 18 kDa, 21 kDa, 28 kDa, 30 kDa, 39 kDa, 41 kDa, 45 kDa, 58 kDa, 66 kDa, 93 kDa, or two out of three bands on IgM: 24 kDa, 39 kDa, 41 kDa. This, along with a clinical diagnosis, with symptoms of only an arthritic bad knee.

I was nine bands IgM positive, which meant a current infection, and IgG negative, which means it wasn't a past infection. Here is

67 Nebbeling, David. *Breaking Grounds on Broken Bones*. Advantage Media Group. 2016.

proof that the regular Western blot test is a joke and should not be used for detecting Lyme disease. All insurance companies should cover the cost of the IGeneX test, and the FDA should approve the Darkfield (live cell) microscopy testing. Or, they could go back to the old way to detect Lyme by getting rid of the ELISA test and go back to only requiring a positive IgM 41 kDa on the Western blot test, as Alan Steere identified in 1986.[68] Better yet, start using the only FDA-approved patent test, which Yale owns (#5,618,533), that is for a specific recombinant fragment of Borrelia burgdorferi flagellin. Then, change back the case definition to relapsing fever, neurological Lyme post-sepsis or cross-tolerance, so people can get disability and the care they need. More on this in Chapter 10.

Dr. Nebbeling gave me my second round of neurotherapy and agreed to try IV hydrogen peroxide on me the following day.

Before Dr. Nebbeling had me as a patient, he didn't see too many people diagnosed with Lyme disease. He had attended a seminar on Lyme disease and had just returned from it the day my test came back. He shared with me other methods people were using to get better, and had heard about H2O2 (hydrogen peroxide); he was willing to give it a go. Dr. Nebbeling felt UVBI was a good place to start and that I should do IV vitamin C with a shot of glutathione along with an ozone push. Dr. Nebbeling also heard about doctors giving IV silver for Lyme with great success.

According to Dr. Easterling, before your doctor starts giving you high doses of vitamin C they should run a blood test to check for a glucose-6-phosphate dehydrogenase (G6PD) deficiency. Even

[68] "Antigens of Borrelia Burgdorferi Recognized during Lyme Disease. Appearance of a New Immunoglobulin M Response and Expansion of the Immunoglobulin G Response Late in the Illness." *The Journal of Clinical Investigation.* U.S. National Library of Medicine. Web. <https://www.ncbi.nlm.nih.gov/pubmed/3531237>

though it is very rare, it can be fatal because it damages the red blood cells. If one has G6PD, they should only do IV hydrogen peroxide instead of high doses of vitamin C.

When doctors are willing to study and learn about your disease and learn new ways to make you better, this is a great sign that you are seeing a good doctor. The reason why Dr. Nebbeling didn't see too many people with Lyme disease was because it is incredibly difficult to get the diagnosis. More than likely, Dr. Nebbeling, and any other health care physician or holistic healer, has treated a lot of people with Lyme disease and wasn't aware of it because it mimics over 350 diseases.

I texted my husband to let him know the results of the IGeneX test. Let's just say, he wasn't impressed or sold that it was accurate. Regardless, he told me if I stopped my treatments, he would buy me a new wardrobe and a new car. I was furious that he somehow had money for a car and a new wardrobe for me, but no funds for my holistic treatments. I didn't care about the material things. I just wanted to get better. Health before wealth!

While there are many doubters in the medical world and possibly in your personal life, there are also some great health care physicians and holistic healers who can help with your treatment. Go to my *Life Healing Handbook* at **www.OvercomingLymeDisease.com/free-handbook** to learn more about the treatments that have helped me overcome Lyme.

CHAPTER 8

Double Standard

"In the fullness of time, the mainstream handling of chronic Lyme disease will be viewed as one of the most shameful episodes in the history of medicine because elements of academic medicine, elements of government and virtually the entire insurance industry have colluded to deny a disease."
–Dr. K. Liegner

The CDC and insurance companies don't recognize Lyme disease unless you have a clinical diagnosis and a confirmed blood test that they accept. Clinical meaning you have a bull's eye rash with symptoms of just an arthritic bad knee. Unfortunately, it is a crime that the "Powers that Be" allow doctors to diagnose their patients with chronic fatigue, lupus, fibromyalgia, chronic pain, etc., based on symptoms only, but they don't allow the same for Lyme disease. Maybe we are onto something here.

Why on earth are they not allowing doctors to diagnose Lyme disease based on symptoms? Other than there is no money in it for them right now? Maybe it is because they have no safe vaccine or man-made drug that will work? Plus, there could be a darker or more diabolical reason why. More on this in Chapter 10.

Denied Bloodwork in ER

Up until now, I thought the reason why I wasn't tested for Lyme disease after falling mysteriously ill two years ago was because I didn't have a tick attached to me, with red lines around the bite spot symbolizing infection. Ha! I was WRONG!

Apparently, you can have part of a tick attached to you, with clear indications of infection, and doctors aren't even worried or thinking that there is a remote chance that you could be getting infected by Lyme or any of the co-infections that ride along with Lyme disease. I witnessed this firsthand when I recently took my brother Richie to the ER to remove a tick that had been embedded in his belly button for at least a couple weeks.

Richie thought that the spot in his belly button was a skin mole. It wasn't. Until it started to grow in size and cause extreme pain in his stomach area, he didn't even consider that it might be something else. His girlfriend looked at it, and together they tried to remove it with rubbing alcohol, oil and tweezers. The body broke off instead, leaving the head attached to his body. The broken body of the tick was filled with dark blood.

They did what the CDC recommended at CDC.org. The CDC also tells you to flush the tick down the toilet.[69] Really? How do you know if it has Lyme disease?

Within ten minutes, Richie felt like throwing up. Severe pain radiated at the bite spot and caused his joints in his upper body to ache. A couple of weeks prior, Richie had started feeling fatigue,

---

69 "Tick Removal and Testing." *Centers for Disease Control and Prevention.* Centers for Disease Control and Prevention, 05 Nov. 2015. Web.

headaches, and flu-like symptoms that left his joints aching like his arthritis had moved to other parts of his body.

Once I told the ER doctor that I overcame Lyme disease holistically after I was misdiagnosed for several years, the doctor got an attitude with me. He questioned that I even had Lyme disease and asked me what doctor treated me and what I did to heal. He then told us that ticks are not out at this time of year. I asked him to look at the tick in my brother's belly button. He said he would get to that later.

After giving my brother a full physical, he finally looked at his belly button. Richie gritted his teeth in extreme pain when the doctor touched the red infected site and the head of the embedded tick. The doctor asked my brother what the tick looked like. When Richie told him that it had grown to the size of his small thumbnail, the doctor said that particular size tick doesn't carry Lyme disease. I wanted to laugh at his ignorance, but this was not a laughing matter!

The ER doctor then said he needed to surgically remove the tick head and that he was going to talk to an infectious disease doctor. When he came back into the room, he said that the ID doc said to give Richie one day of doxycycline, an antibiotic. I asked the doctor if he would run blood work, and he happily chanted that Lyme disease is hard to diagnose and that the current blood tests don't detect it.

The doctor proceeded to numb my brother's stomach to surgically remove the tick. Once he pulled it out and cleaned the area, he said that he was going to give Richie a week of doxycycline and pain meds, since there was sign of infection. I asked the doctor one more time to please order any type of blood work to see how bad his infection was. The doctor laughed and said, "There is infection, and there is infection." I thought, "What does that mean, and do people really buy into this BS?"

My brother got dressed and we left the ER.

Richie took the antibiotics. He was still not feeling well. He has become very lethargic, irritable, and his pain has increased. Hmm, those symptoms sound familiar! As you can see, the medical community is obviously misinformed as to what Lyme disease really is, thanks to the CDC and the "Powers that Be."

Don't Give into Your Fears!

"Our doubts are traitors and make us lose the good
we might oft win by fearing to attempt or stop mid-course."
–William Shakespeare

Dr. Nebbeling wanted me to do ten big bags of IV vitamin C with ozone, along with alternating days with IV H2O2. So, I started the IV vitamin C treatment the following day. Before then, I was able to drive myself. The treatment made me extremely tired and weak. Driving home that day, I fell asleep at the wheel. Thankfully, I woke up right away with no accident.

Falling asleep driving scared me enough to ask family and friends for help taking me to my appointments. I didn't want to impose on anyone, but I had no choice. I was worried that if I asked for help, it would be too inconvenient for them or they would say no since it was an hour drive both ways and/or maybe they believed that the treatment I was seeking was quackery.

I had to have courage to be my own advocate if I was going to get better. Desire or pain is what makes us all step out and overcome whatever problems we are facing. As you can see, I had both of them working for me here. I had desire to get better, and I had pain in every category.

God must have heard my prayers. When I reached out to family and friends, they wanted to help me! It felt so good to have others care and be a part of my healing. I was humbled and extremely grateful. A huge thank you to: Kim Ellicott, Anita Linden Belmore, Lynn Boham, Cathy Issel, Carol Darr, Trish Ruikka, Sharon Scoffins, Karen and Richard Easterling, Teddy Darr, and Cindy Scappaticci. These men and women had to travel far and wait for four to five hours while I was getting my IV treatments. I am forever grateful!

More Doctors Fired!

I continued my treatments and my right jaw started hurting really badly. I went back to the biological dentist who had removed my mercury fillings and complained. He said the x-rays looked great! I asked if he could send me to a specialist for a second opinion, so he sent me to an endodontist.

The endodontist said that three of my root canals were bad and infected. He said that I needed two of them re-done and the third root canal tooth, which showed a major abscess, needed to be removed and replaced with an implant.

I told him about Lyme disease and that root canals aren't good, especially with Lyme; I just wanted them removed. He then told me that his niece has Lyme disease and her parents are doctors. They were renting a house in FL and were paying cash so their daughter could get IV antibiotics for the last year. I guess they were spending $100,000 a year to treat her. That sounds about right for a person battling Lyme disease.

I told my endodontist that antibiotics will not help and perhaps they should look into oxygen therapies and find a wise naturopathic doctor or chiropractor who knows how to treat the body. Let's just say, that didn't go over too well! So, once again, I got to be like Donald Trump in the old TV show, *The Apprentice*. I fired my biological dentist and endodontist. It is very important to remember, you do have the power to fire your doctors if you don't agree with them and when you don't think they can handle the job of helping you.

Dr. Easterling likes to say, "Doctors go to medical school and then they open a 'practice,' and that is what they do, they 'practice' medicine." In other words, they don't heal the body, they only cover up symptoms with synthetic drugs. Too bad we aren't synthetic. I am a firm believer now that his statement is totally true.

Dr. Nebbeling was shocked to hear his friend would not remove the root canal tooth. He brainstormed and remembered meeting this smart, energetic dentist in Milan, named Dr. Natalie Horn. Dr. Horn said she was aware of how root canals can be dangerous to your body. She had studied and knew how each tooth affected different organs and systems in the body, hence the name of her office, Meridian Dentistry.

Very few dentists know that "every one of the 32 spots in our jaw is directly connected to organs in our body, whether you have a tooth there or not."[70]

Did you know that there was a medical study published by the Independent Cancer Research Foundation to see if there is any correlation between breast cancer and root canals? The results will

---

[70] "The Truth About Cancer: A Global Quest - Episode Five." *Cancer Tutor.* 08 Nov. 2016. Web. <https://www.cancertutor.com/ttac-global-quest-cancer-blind-spots-toxic-vaccines-homeopathy-emotions/>

shock you: 98% women with breast cancer had at least one root canal tooth:

Dr. Thomas Rau, who runs the Paracelsus Clinic (cancer clinic since 1958) in Switzerland recently checked the records of the last 150 breast cancer patients treated in his clinic. He found that 147 of them (98%) had one or more root canal teeth on the same meridian as the original breast cancer tumor. His clinic has a biological dentist section where all cancer patients, on reporting in, have their mouth cleaned up first -- especially all root canal teeth removed.

There are about 24 million root canals done in the U.S. alone every year. They were proven deadly disease agents in 1925 in a study by Dr. Weston Price and 60 prominent researchers. That study has been suppressed ever since by the ADA and the American Association of Endodontists (AAE). Read the book "Root Canal Cover-Up" by George Meinig, DDS, FACD for the full story. Dr. Meinig was an endodontist for 50 years. He helped found the AAE in 1943. His book is a mea culpa (apology) to the thousands of patients whose health he ruined doing root canal fillings. He discovered the Weston Price research only after he retired in 1993. His book was published first in 1994 and he has lectured widely since then trying to alert people to this danger to their health.[71]

Imagine that, the ADA and the AAE covered up this study. Can someone say, "Shocker"? This shows again that cancer comes

---

[71] The Relationship Between Root Canals and Cancer." *The ICRF | Independent Cancer Research Foundation.* 22 Dec. 2015. Web. <http://www.theicrf.com/Articles/RootCanals/>

from some sort of underlying infection. More on that to come, keep connecting the dots.

New Biological Dentist Hired, Dr. Natalie Horn

I met with Dr. Horn and was totally impressed by all of her degrees: Naturopathic Doctor, Biological Dentist, Herbalist, and Kinesiology, just to name a few. Dr. Horn looked at the x-rays from my endodontist's office and did some muscle testing to see what was really going on. Sure enough, all four were testing bad. Since she could tell by my health state that I was too weak to have all four removed at one time, she decided to remove them one at a time. So, on October 30, 2014, Devil's Night, I had my first infected root canal removed.

During this time, Dr. Easterling and his wife Karen came up from Indiana to stay with us and meet Dr. Nebbeling. I was doing great the night of my first oral surgery. Karen had made me some homemade lentil soup for dinner. I was taking my favorite powerful healing enzymes that Dr. Easterling recommends for severe system problems, including cancer and AIDS. This enzyme formula contains the enzymes protease, amylase, lipase, and disaccharidases, calcium lactate, and kelp, a source of minerals. Enzymes are crucial to your healing. Read Chapter 12, The Crucial Role of Enzymes.

Dr. Horn also had me use a heating pad to help drain the infection. Dr. Horn had me rub Oil of Cajeput (by Pure Herbs, LTD) on my gums for the pain and infection. What I have now recently discovered is how important Oil of Cajeput was for my healing. From Dr. A. B. Howard's book, *Supplement to the copyrighted work Herbal Extracts, Build Better Health with Liquid Herbs*:

Properties and Uses: fungus infections, natural antibiotic oil, yeast, candida, sinus, colds, flu, fever, laryngitis, pain, toothaches and abscesses, ringworm, athletes foot, lice, colitis, vaginal douche, impetigo, skin, boils, carbuncles, external sores, mosquito and insect bites.

Oil of Cajeput comes to us from the tropics of India and the Molucca Islands of Indonesia. This small tree, or tall bush with dropping limbs, is much like a weeping willow, with multiple layers of paper-like-thin bark. Cajeput Oil is related, in function, to something called "Tea tree Oil", but the action, and not unpleasing taste of Cajeput, is preferred by a great many herbalists. In spite of its tropical home in a humid, hot environment, the Cajeput tree does not fall prey to fungus or infections because of the antibiotic oil which circulates in its sap (circulatory fluid). It maintains very good health, thank you.[72]

Wow, it doesn't fall prey to fungus or infections! Hmm, this sounds like something everyone should have in their "medicine cabinet"?

Enough is Enough

I retired early to bed, around 9pm. My husband still wasn't happy about everything I was doing and still did not believe I had Lyme disease.

I am not sure for how long, but I found out that night that my husband's doctor had been prescribing Ambien to help him

---

[72] Howard, Dr. A B. *Supplement to the Copyrighted Work Herbal Extracts, Build Better Health with Liquid Herbs*. 8th ed.: Blue Goose, 2001. Print.

115

sleep. Unfortunately, if you don't take it as prescribed, it causes blackouts. In a drugged, sleepwalking state, my husband angrily paced the house violently threatening me and breaking things. The events that had happened that night were not the first. It was just my last! I had finally realized that I could no longer live with an unsupportive husband, who didn't trust or believe in me.

What toxic relationships are you still holding on to?

In the morning, my husband left for work like normal. I was devastated and frightened by what had happened during the night and embarrassed that my doctor and his wife witnessed some of it. I went downstairs to say goodbye to Rich and Karen before they left for home. When I shared with them my fears, they offered to help me pack up and leave for some place safe. So, I called my dear friend, Kim Ellicott and she said, "Come over, you can stay here." Karen, Rich and I then loaded up our vehicles with some of my personal belongings and we drove to Kim's.

During this time, I had finally had enough and filed for a divorce. I truly was afraid that my husband would put me in a mental institute since he had my power of attorney and the CDC promotes you are cured with one round of antibiotics. I reasoned that he would be able to say I was treated and I still am "acting" sick, therefore I must be crazy!

For the next two months, I continued to drive an hour each way to get my IV oxygen therapies, neuro-therapy and prolotherapy from Dr. Nebbeling. I stayed mostly at Kim's home, but did stay at times with my brother Richie and my friend, Anita Belmore. If I can live house to house and fight this disease, you can, too! The secret is to not

give up! Believe anything is possible and that
your healing is around the corner!
Get your copy of my *Life Healing Handbook* at
www.OvercomingLymeDisease.com/free-handbook
to learn recipes that can help you heal!

CHAPTER 9

The Militarization of Public Health in the 21st Century

"A single vaccine given to a six-pound newborn is the equivalent of giving a 180-pound adult 30 vaccinations on the same day."
–Dr. Boyd Haley, Toxicologist and Retired Professor of Chemistry, University of Kentucky

It is sad that California just voted in a bill that mandates all children that want to attend public school must be fully vaccinated. I am talking about a bill that is forcing children that had become autistic, paralyzed, developed seizures, etc., after receiving a vaccine to continue to get vaccines if they want to attend public school. The only exception is IF their doctor will report that their negative response was caused by the vaccine. This is extremely hard to do because doctors are being pressured not to report them, under threat of losing their medical license. Big Pharma must be super excited about this one!

So, no matter what your state of health is in, you must get fully vaccinated. They are selling this crazy idea on the premise that it is for the greater good of the public. Your personal rights to say what goes in your body no longer count. It is sort of like what they do with cancer. If your child has cancer, you have no say in their treatments. You must use the cancer-causing, barbaric protocols that are proven to fail: chemo, radiation, and surgery.

From the website National Vaccine Information Center:

Get Vaccinated, Homeschool or Go To Jail?

California now becomes one of only three states, along with West Virginia and Mississippi, that denies children entry to daycare and school unless they get dozens of doses of federally recommended vaccines or a medical doctor grants a medical vaccine exemption, an exemption that doctors deny to 99.99 percent of children under narrow federal guidelines. Parents who do not comply with the new law will have to homeschool their children and, if they cannot homeschool for financial or other reasons, they may be subject to truancy laws that include fines and imprisonment for failing to provide their children with an education.[73]

As I have shared information on the topic of the dangers of vaccines on social media and in daily conversations with family and friends, a lot of people say, "But the polio vaccine wiped out polio."

Actually, via good sanitary practices and good nutrition, polio disappeared. Not to mention, the polio vaccine contained a tainted, cancer-causing virus, SV40, which was injected into ninety-eight million Americans.[74] Still trusting the vaccine manufacturers?

---

[73]   "California Enacts SB277 Despite Human & Civil Rights Concerns - NVIC Newsletter." *National Vaccine Information Center (NVIC)*. Web. <http://www.nvic.org/nvic-vaccine-news/july-2015/california-sb277-enacted-end-medical-tryanny.aspx>

[74]   Cancer Risk Associated with Simian Virus 40 Contaminated Polio Vaccine." *Anticancer Research*. U.S. National Library of Medicine. Web.

Here are some of the cancers that the polio vaccine has caused:[75]

Brain Cancers	Astrocytoma	Bone Cancers	Osteosarcoma
	Anaplastic Astrocytoma		Ewing's Tumors
	Choroid Plexus Papilloma	Chest Cancers	
	Ependymoma		Mesothelioma
	Gemistocytic Astrocytoma	Lymphomas	Non-Hodgkins Lymphoma (NHL)
	Glioblastoma		
	Gliosarcoma	Thyroid Cancers	Papillary thyroid carcinomas
	Medulloblastoma		
	Meningioma		Anaplastic thyroid carcinomas (ATC)
	Oligodendroglioma		
	Pituitary Adenoma		

Back in the day, vaccine manufacturers took responsibility for their deadly vaccines, because they didn't have a law that protected them. According to the SV40 Foundation, "In 1960, the pharmaceutical company Merck & Co. wrote to the U.S. Surgeon General:

Our scientific staff have emphasized to us that there are a number of serious scientific and technical problems that must be solved before we could engage in large-scale production of live poliovirus vaccine. Most important among these is the problem of extraneous contaminating simian viruses that may be extremely difficult to eliminate and which may be difficult if not impossible to detect at the present stage of the technology."[76]

---

[75] "Types of SV40 Cancers." *Types of SV40 Cancers*. Web.
<http://www.sv40foundation.org/Types.html>

[76] "SV40-Cancer-Polio Vaccine Link." *SV40-Cancer-Polio Vaccine Link*. Web.
<http://www.sv40foundation.org/cpv-link.html>

The Startling Increase in Vaccines Given to Children

In 1983, the American children received only ten doses of vaccines from birth to six years of age.[77]

Here is the list:

DTP (2 months)	DTP- Diphtheria, Tetanus, Pertussis (whole cell)
OPV (2 months)	OPV- Oral Polio
DTP (4 months)	MMR- Measles, Mumps, Rubella
OPV (4 months)	Hep B- Hepatitis B
DTP (6 months)	DTaP-Diphtheria, Tetanus, Pertussis (acellular)
MMR (15 months)	HIB- Haemophilus influenza Type B
DTP (18 months)	PCV- Pneumococcal
OPV (18 months)	IPV- Inactivated Polio
DTP (48 months)	Varicella – Chicken Pox
OPV (48 months)	

In 1986, The National Childhood Vaccine Injury Act was passed. It was to protect pharmaceutical companies from the growing tide of vaccine-injured children. Under this law, no parent can sue a vaccine manufacturer. What? How could this law have passed? They passed a law to prevent the "drug cartel" from being sued because their vaccines were injuring children? Everyone should be outraged about this one! I guess this is why there is a growing population of caring and injured citizens who aren't going to be brainwashed anymore.

Who says there is no money in pharmaceuticals? Check out the number of vaccines Big Pharma is now recommending. Each

---

[77] "CDC Mandatory Vaccine Schedule: 1983 vs 2013 - Vermont Coalition for Vaccine Choice" -. Web. <http://www.vaxchoicevt.com/2013/03/26/cdc-mandatory-vaccine-schedule-1983-vs-2013/>

year a new standard has been put in place, increasing the number of vaccines. As of 2015, an American child receives at least thirty vaccines in their first six years of life. Here is the list from the CDC:[78]

Influenza (Pregnancy)	HIB (12 months)
DTaP (Pregnancy)	PCV (12 months)
Hep B (birth)	MMR (12 months)
Rotavirus (2 months)	Varicella (12 months)
DTaP (2 months)	Hep A (18 months)
HIB (2 months)	Influenza (30 months)
PCV (2 months)	Influenza (42 months)
IPV (2 months)	DTaP (48 months)
Rotavirus (6 months)	IPV (48 months)
DTaP (6 months)	MMR (48 months)
HIB (6 months)	Varicella (48 months)
PCV (6 months)	Influenza (60 months)
IPV (6 months)	Influenza (72 months)
Influenza (6 months)	

Because the drug companies are protected by law, these vaccines are unregulated and carry dangerous toxins. The three main toxins added to vaccines, other than the unknown bacteria-fungi, and the animal viruses that should never be injected into humans, are: aluminum, mercury, and formaldehyde.[79] Aluminum and mercury are neurotoxins, they wreak havoc on our nervous system and brain. Aluminum greatly increases the toxicity of mercury, even in small

---

78 http://www.cdc.gov/vaccines/schedules/downloads/child/0-18yrs-child-combined-schedule.pdf

79 "SV40-Cancer-Polio Vaccine Link." *SV40-Cancer-Polio Vaccine Link*. Web. <http://www.sv40foundation.org/cpv-link.html>

amounts. In 2011, the US National Toxicology Program described formaldehyde as "known to be a human carcinogen."[80] The kicker here is you don't know how much of these deadly toxins are in each vaccine!

The drug companies have been placing these toxins in their vaccines since the 1930s. One reason they use aluminum is that it jolts the body's immune system. Well, that is not the only thing it jolts! It has been linked to Alzheimer's disease, epilepsy, asthma, hyperactivity, and Down's syndrome. Besides that, there has never been adequate clinical research to prove it is safe.[81]

What Is Thimerosal?

Let's see what the FDA says about thimerosal:

> Thimerosal is a mercury-containing organic compound (an organomercurial). Since the 1930s, it has been widely used as a preservative in a number of biological and drug products, including many vaccines, to help prevent potentially life threatening contamination with harmful microbes. Over the past several years, because of an increasing awareness of the theoretical potential for neurotoxicity of even low levels of organomercurials and because of the increased number of thimerosal containing vaccines that had been added to the infant immunization schedule, concerns about the use of

---

[80] *National Institutes of Health.* U.S. Department of Health and Human Services. Web. <http://www.niehs.nih.gov/news/newsroom/releases/2011/june10/>

[81] "Aluminum and Vaccine Ingredients – National Vaccine Information Center." *National Vaccine Information Center (NVIC).* Web. <http://www.nvic.org/Doctors-Corner/Aluminum-and-Vaccine-Ingredients.aspx>

thimerosal in vaccines and other products have been raised. Indeed, because of these concerns, the Food and Drug Administration has worked with, and continues to work with, vaccine manufacturers to reduce or eliminate thimerosal from vaccines.

Thimerosal has been removed from or reduced to trace amounts in all vaccines routinely recommended for children 6 years of age and younger, with the exception of the inactivated influenza vaccine. A preservative-free version of inactivated influenza vaccine (contains trace amounts of thimerosal) is available in limited supply at this time for use in infants, children and pregnant women. Some vaccines such as Td, which is indicated for older children ($\geq$ 7 years of age) and adults are also now available in formulations that are free of thimerosal or contain only trace amounts. Vaccines with trace amounts of thimerosal contain 1 microgram or less of mercury per dose.[82]

Interesting! The FDA says thimerosal is added to vaccines "to help prevent potentially life threatening contamination with harmful microbes." Are they admitting to the fact that vaccines can be contaminated with something that is harmful to you?

Did you notice that in 2001, they finally stopped using thimerosal in children's vaccines because they were hurting so many kids via the mercury poison? Too bad they can't stop the threat of the vaccine being contaminated with "harmful microbes." However, they are still using thimerosal in the flu vaccine that they give to children, pregnant women and adults.

---

82   "Thimerosal in Vaccines." *Thimerosal in Vaccines.* Web.

Triplets Develop Autism from Vaccine

My dear friend, Marian Van Calbi, whom I met through Silpada Designs, had this awful reaction happen to all three of her triplets. Right after their eighteen-month MMR (Measles, Mumps and Rubella) vaccination, all three of them developed Autism.

It is easy to say it isn't the vaccine when one child has this reaction, but when all three? Obviously, they were already immunosuppressed or the vaccine made them that way by being contaminated with something.

The CDC even says that their vaccines fail by giving people the very diseases they allegedly prevent.[83] The CDC says that immunosuppressed children should not get certain live vaccines.[84] Unfortunately, they don't test for immunosuppression before they vaccinate, and it would be hard to know if you are just coming down with a cold that would cause immunosuppression. Mixed with brain-tropic viruses, like in MMR vaccine, children are becoming Autistic.

The Advisory Committee on Immunization Practices (ACIP) even says not to vaccinate immunosuppressed children. "Updated information on adverse events and contraindications, particularly for persons with severe HIV infection, persons with egg allergy or gelatin allergy, persons with a history of thrombocytopenia, and persons receiving steroid therapy."[85] Notice the egg or gelatin allergy? This explains why my daughter always got sick with her mandated vaccines. More proof on this in Chapter 10.

---

[83] Artenstein, Andrew W. *Vaccines: A Biography*. New York: Springer, 2010. Print.

[84] https://www.cdc.gov/vaccines/Pubs/pinkbook/downloads/prinvac.pdf

[85] *Centers for Disease Control and Prevention*. Centers for Disease Control and Prevention. Web. <https://www.cdc.gov/mmwr/preview/mmwrhtml/00053391.htm>

In December 2013, the court awarded Ryan B. Mojabi $969,474.91 for developing autism from the MMR Vaccine. There are numerous cases like this happening daily, but you won't hear about it in the news since it would shed light on our failed "sick care" system.[86]

Quick tip if you don't live in California, West Virginia, or Mississippi, you can still claim religion as a reason to waive the requirements to have your child vaccinated. Up until now most hospital staff, doctors, nurses, police officers, firemen, and our military could not claim religion as a reason not to get the flu vaccine, unless they wanted to lose their job. A recent Federal Law ruled in favor of health care professionals being able to claim religion.

In late 2013 and early 2014, six employees of Saint Vincent Hospital refused to have flu shots—on religious grounds—and were fired. The hospital has now agreed to rehire them and provide about $300,000 in back pay and compensatory damages, as part of a settlement for a lawsuit that was filed, on behalf of the workers, by the Equal Employment Opportunity Commission in September.

The commission claimed that the hospital had violated Title VII of the Civil Rights Act of 1964 when it fired the employees. Although the hospital had implemented a mandatory flu vaccination policy for all employees, they had granted medical exemptions to 14 other workers.[87]

---

[86] http://www.uscfc.uscourts.gov/sites/default/files/opinions/CAMPBELL-SMITH.MOJA-BI-PROFFER.12.13.2012.pdf

[87] "Erie Hospital to Pay, Rehire Workers Who Refused Vaccines." *Health Nut News*. 24 Dec. 2016. Web. <http://www.healthnutnews.com/hospital-rehire-workers-flu-shot/>

Paralyzed from Gardasil Vaccine

Another dear friend of mine's oldest daughter, Kortney Meadows, became ill after her third dose of Gardasil vaccine, the one that is supposed to protect you from cervical cancer. She was in her first year of college, had the world in her hands, and she was healthy. Here is her story:

> In 2009, after I got my last and final Gardasil vaccination, a couple weeks later I had a rash show up on my right thigh. After using Benadryl because that's what my Dr. suggested it went away, within a week I started having double vision. That double vision lasted for a while. My right arm and left leg then became numb and then my right leg and left arm. I was admitted into the hospital. Test after test was given to me and nothing was found. My neurologist then diagnosed me with idiopathic transverse myelitis, which that means inflammation of the spine but they don't know why. I was in the hospital for 4 days. I walked into the hospital and 4 days later came out in a wheelchair because I was paralyzed. Worst experience of my life and if I knew all the damage this vaccination could do to me I would have never thought of getting it. Trying to protect myself from cervical cancer led to 7 years of struggle and fighting.

Due to getting this vaccine and not knowing if she was developing a cold, or if the vaccine was contaminated, Kortney became immunosuppressed. Kortney was tested for Lyme in the hospital, but the results came back positive/negative; whatever that means...

By the way, did you know most insurance companies offer health care providers incentives for vaccinating their patients? Blue Cross Blue Shield pays pediatricians $400 per child if they vaccinate 63% of their patients with all their suggested vaccines by age two. If they don't hit the 63% mark, they don't get their bonus.[88] This is horrible!

Why Are Top Holistic Doctors Dying?

If you are a Christian, this next story may sound familiar. It reminds me of when Christ was born in the manger, and the "Powers that Be" ordered all firstborn sons up to two years of age to be murdered. Sort of like what they are doing with all of the smart Holistic Doctors that have figured out how to heal the body and were ready to expose the truth about what they found was being added to vaccines. So far, the "Powers that Be" are winning, but remember the TRUTH always comes out![89]

In the article by Julie Wilson, staff writer: "REVEALED: Cancer Industry Profits 'Locked In' by Nagalase Molecule Injected into Humans via Vaccines... Spurs Tumor Growth... Explains Aggressive Vaccine Push" from July 27, 2015, it talks about how cancer is a $100 billion dollar profitable industry and how the "Powers that Be" don't want to find a cure because they would lose all of this money and be out of a job.

---

88 http://www.whale.to/c/2016-BCN-BCBSM-Incentive-Program-Booklet.pdf

89 "Dead Doctors and the GcMAF Connection - Dr. James Jeffrey Bradstreet (RIP) - Dr. Nicholas Gonzalez (RIP) - Vaccine Mafia's Intimidation Tactics - Cancer Industry's Arrogant Racketeering - Disease-Causing Nagalase Introduced Intentionally Either Virally or Through Vaccines? - Curing Autism and Cancer - Medical Villains Failing to Achieve Their Endgame." *Abel Danger*. Web.

The article shares how top holistic doctors that have successfully treated patients with cancer and autism are being raided by the FDA because they have been using a protein that reverses the damage being done by this nagalase molecule. Not only are they being raided, but they have been mysteriously dying. The article shares how these doctors have discovered the nagalase molecule, which vaccine makers are injecting into humans, is causing immune suppression. This makes them a huge threat to the "Powers that Be."

From the article "REVEALED: Cancer Industry Profits 'Locked In' by Nagalase Molecule Injected into Humans via Vaccines... Spurs Tumor Growth... Explains Aggressive Vaccine Push": [90]

Doctor compares cancer-causing nagalase to stealth bomber

Nagalase blocks the GC protein from attaching itself to vitamin D, thus preventing the immune system from doing its job and therefore causing cancer and other serious diseases. Without an active immune system, cancer and viral infections can spread rapidly.

Remarkably, there's a significant amount of research available on nagalase and the GcMAF protein. Citing a chapter from *The GcMAF Book* by Dr. Tim Smith, MD, Dr. Broer said:

Nagalase is like a stealth bomber, the nagalase enzyme synthesized in or released from cancer cells or a virus particle pinpoints the GcMAF protein facilities on the surface of your T and B lymphocytes and simply wipes them out with an incredibly precise bomb.

---

[90] "REVEALED: Cancer Industry Profits 'locked In' by Nagalase Molecule Injected into Humans via Vaccines... Spurs Tumor Growth... Explains Aggressive Vaccine Push." *NaturalNews*. Web. <http://www.naturalnews.com/050582_nagalase_GcMAF_cancer_industry_profits.html>

How precise? Nagalase locates and attacks one specific two-electron bond located only at the 420th amino acid position on a huge protein molecule, one of tens of thousands of proteins, each containing millions of electrons.

This is like selectively taking out a park bench in a major city from 6,000 miles away. More astonishingly, if that is possible, nagalase never misses its target, so there is no collateral damage.[91]

Bradshaw and all of the deceased holistic doctors believed they were injecting this immune suppressor in vaccines. For more information and research on GcMAF, go to http://www.saisei-mirai.or.jp/gan/macrophage_colostrum_gcmaf_eng.html

In the next chapter, we will focus on how this relates to the fake/failed LYMErix vaccine.

From the information in this chapter, it is clear that vaccines should be avoided. To learn about other dangers to be avoided, go to my *Life Healing Handbook* at **www.OvercomingLymeDisease.com/free-handbook**.

---

[91]   "The GcMAF Book." *The GcMAF Book.* Web. <http://gcmaf.timsmithmd.com/book/book/4/all/>

CHAPTER 10

Failed LYMErix Vaccine

*"It's easier to fool people than to convince them
that they have been fooled."*
–Mark Twain

id you know that the CDC already had a "vaccine" for
Lyme disease? Supposedly, it got pulled off the market
because there wasn't a "high enough demand for it." Yeah, right!
The LYMErix (OspA) patent holder at Yale University (patent
#5,747,294), CDC offi cers, and others who were in bed with them
for the commercialization of OspA (ALDF, Mayo Clinic, Yale's L2
Diagnostics, Corixa, Imugen, SmithKline) lied to the FDA about
the testing and manipulated the studies during case trials for the
vaccine. It wasn't on the market for long before Kathleen Dickson,
a chemist at Pfizer, blew the whistle to the Department Of Justice
(DOJ) about how these elite CDC members changed the proper
testing for Lyme and she showed the DOJ how OspA causes
immune suppression, rather than it being a vaccine that they
claimed it to be.[92] The FDA asked the makers to pull LYMErix off
the market, or they would. Hmm... something sounds fishy here!

---

[92]   http://www.fda.gov/ohrms/dockets/ac/01/slides/3680s2_11.pdf

In order to manipulate the success rate of the LYMErix vaccine adult trial, the CDC crooks lied to the FDA about their new testing, which added the ELISA total antibody concentration test, and dumbed down the original Western blot test in order to sell their fake vaccine and testing kits. This is known as the Dearborn Stunt that took place in 1994 in Dearborn, MI. The original Western blot test tested for OspA and OspB, (Outer surface protein of the same plasmid, bands 31 and 34).

They used this strain with no lipids in the testing because they didn't want an antibody response, which would show up on the ELISA. Without an antibody response, CDC says you don't have the disease. Of course, they didn't want the disease showing up in their testing patients. That would make the vaccine a failure, especially when your vaccine is the disease, which makes it not a vaccine.

Once LYMErix was on the market, the CDC said you can't send your blood work to any other lab but theirs: Yale's L2 Diagnostics, Corixa and Imugen. They wanted everyone to send their blood work to their labs to test for Lyme disease so they could discover new vector-borne diseases and patent them for future vaccines and testing kits. Could someone say racketeering?

How the Crime Happened

In 1994 during the FDA meeting for the Lyme vaccine, Dr. Raymond Dattwyler protested and said that Steere and the CDC were wrong. The case definition of only a bad knee is not true and the sickest people with Lyme disease are seronegative, meaning they have no antibody response. Regardless, the FDA approved the falsified case definition and testing methods, because top officials at the CDC lied to the FDA.

Dattwyler wrote in 1988 with the Department of Medicine, State of University of New York, School of Medicine, Stony Brook, about how the sickest people with Lyme disease have no antibody response and they have more health issues than an arthritic bad knee. This article, "Seronegative Lyme Disease. Dissociation of Specific T- and B-lymphocyte Responses to Borrelia burgdorferi" concluded that "the presence of chronic Lyme disease cannot be excluded by the absence of antibodies against B. burgdorferi and that a specific T-cell blastogenic response to B. burgdorferi is evidence of infection in seronegative patients with clinical indications of chronic Lyme disease."[93]

This was written two years before Alan Barbour and his cronies started their fake non-profit, called American Lyme Disease Foundation (ALDF.com), to spin the disease to the world.

Again, two years before ALDF was formed, in 1988, Dattwyler also helped write a report with the Department of Medicine, State University of New York, School of Medicine, Stony Brook, called, "Modulation of Natural Killer Cell Activity by Borrelia burgdorferi." In the report, he says that Lyme is seronegative, meaning it doesn't produce antibodies.[94]

---

[93] "Seronegative Lyme Disease. Dissociation of Specific T- and B-lymphocyte Responses to Borrelia Burgdorferi." *The New England Journal of Medicine*. U.S. National Library of Medicine. Web. <https://www.ncbi.nlm.nih.gov/pubmed/3054554>

[94] "Suppression of Natural Killer Cells in Chronic Lyme (an Immunosuppression Disease and Not an Inflammatory Disease)." *Suppression of Natural Killer Cells in Chronic Lyme (an Immunosuppression Disease and Not an Inflammatory Disease)*. Web. <http://www.action-lyme.org/DATTWYLER_NK_SUPPRESSION.htm>

So what is the purpose of the Dearborn stunt where they changed the case definition and the testing for Lyme disease? Excellent question! Did I mention cancer is a $100 billion industry? It all boils down to money! The crooks at the CDC wanted a monopoly on vector-borne disease money, blood, grants, and DNA so they could patent new vector-borne diseases, once LYMErix or OspA was on the market. They had three labs that they said were the only labs that you could send your blood too, Yale's L2 Diagnostics, Corixa and Imugen. Go to www.OvercomingLymeDisease.com for a link to Truth Cures for the full Lyme Crime. This book only includes parts of the story.

What is OspA?

OspA is a fungal antigen that makes up the outer surface protein of (Lyme/Borrelia) spirochetes. Spirochetes shed their outer surface protein to avoid attacks from the immune system. The spirochetes bomb your immune system with this fungal antigen, making you immune-suppressed. This allows common latent viruses of all kinds to become un-latent. How diabolical is this? They put a deadly fungal agent in the vaccine on purpose!

History of the Lyme Crime

In 1990, certain CDC members, including Alan Barbour, who is an OspA vaccine patent holder started, with others, the fake non-profit called ALDF (America Lyme Disease Foundation). The reason why they started the ALDF was to spin the disease and lie to the world about what it really was, in order to sell their fake Lyme vaccine and testing kits. Plus, they wanted to trash their victims in public, which is a color of law criminal charge.

On May 26, 1992, CDC officers William Gould, Joseph Piesman and Barbara Johnson, along with others and SmithKline Beecham Corp., applied for a patent on new Lyme Test Kits. It was approved in 1993 as patent number W09324145.

In 1993, the first clinical trials for the Lyme vaccine had already begun. CDC officer Barbara Johnson had already sent CDC officer Allen Steere to Europe in 1992-1993 to falsify and change the case definition as to what Lyme disease was. Steere changed the case definition from relapsing fever to anyone just having an arthritic bad knee. By doing this, he excluded all of the neurological Lyme (aka post-sepsis or cross-tolerance) outcomes, which included relapsing fevers.

Around this time, the innocent volunteers in the first case study for the Lyme vaccine started to report symptoms of neurological Lyme or post-sepsis. Perfect time to throw a conference to change the testing. The CDC crooks (Barbara Johnson and Alan Steere) lied to the FDA and changed the way testing is done for Lyme with the new case definition for Lyme disease in 1994 at the Second National Conference of Serologic Diagnosis of Lyme Disease in Dearborn, MI. This testing does not meet the FDA standards for method validation (specifically sensitivity, etc.).[95]

---

[95]   Reliosis, Beaux. "Lyme Cryme: How It All Went Down." *Prosecute the Lyme Crooks*. 16 Jan. 2017. Web.

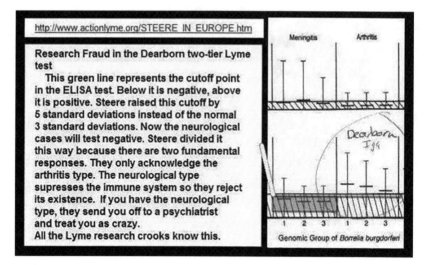

Immune suppression from Lyme disease was defined out of existence through research fraud in designing the Dearborn two-tier test.

With these new changes, they were able to lie to the FDA and make their vaccine look 90% safe and effective:

- new case definition of only a "bad knee,"
- making people first test positive to the ELISA test, which less than 15% of the population has an antibody response to,
- making it harder to test positive on the Western blot test by raising the level of IgG bands and lowering the level of IgM bands needed. The original Western blot only needed new IgM bands to show active infection and only 41-kD to prove you had Lyme.

So, everyone with no antibody response, which shows up as a negative ELISA, were thrown out along with their symptoms or case definition of post-sepsis or neurological Lyme. The sickest were left to suffer and die, and they were not being reported as a failure in the vaccine testing.

This is a crime against humanity! The sickest people are usually the ones with no antibody response. They are the ones that can never get diagnosed and they are left to die with no treatments or financial aid. These Lyme victims can't get disability because they can't prove in court that they have the real case definition of what Lyme disease is, which is relapsing fever, the disease that the CDC says does not exist. This is horrific! Just like the Holocaust!

Earlier Vaccine Trials That Failed Using Fungal Antigens

There were at least three other attempts using another fungal antigen (triacylated lipoprotein) that failed and should have red-flagged anyone from using OspA or OspB as a vaccine. The vaccines were for mycobacterium tuberculosis that caused immune suppression.[96] [97] [98] These trials were done and concluded during the time the ALDF started and when the CDC officers went to Europe to change the case definition for Lyme disease.

---

[96]   "The 19-kD Antigen and Protective Immunity in a Murine Model of Tuberculosis." *Clinical and Experimental Immunology*. U.S. National Library of Medicine. Web. <https://www.ncbi.nlm.nih.gov/pubmed/10792376>

[97]   "Mycobacterium Tuberculosis 19-kilodalton Lipoprotein Inhibits Mycobacterium Smegmatis-induced Cytokine Production by Human Macrophages in Vitro." *Infection and Immunity*. U.S. National Library of Medicine. Web. <https://www.ncbi.nlm.nih.gov/pubmed/11179309>

[98]   Hovav, Avi-Hai, Jacob Mullerad, Liuba Davidovitch, Yolanta Fishman, Fabiana Bigi, Angel Cataldi, and Herve Bercovier. "The *Mycobacterium Tuberculosis* Recombinant 27-Kilodalton Lipoprotein Induces a Strong Th1-Type Immune Response Deleterious to Protection." *Infection and Immunity*. American Society for Microbiology, June 2003. Web. <https://www.ncbi.nlm.nih.gov/pmc/articles/PMC155707/?tool=pubmed>

Meningitis Scandal

There have been many scandals where people were injected with fungi and became ill, and some even died. One incident that I remember is the New England Compounding Center meningitis scandal in 2012.[99] My mother-in-law's husband was extremely worried after he had gotten a steroid injection that made him sick. The injectable steroids in the scandal were fungal contaminated and his doctors didn't know if his was one of them. Because of this, sixty-four people died and close to eight hundred people fell sick from the contaminated steroid.[100] This is proof you can't inject humans with fungi!

Here is the super scary thing—they have known for a while now that vaccines could be contaminated with fungal antigens. That is why they put thimerosal in vaccines, to slow the growth of these triacylated lipoprotein, a TLR2/1 agonist, which acts like a fungal-type antigen. According to the whistleblower on LYMErix, Kathleen Dickson, a former analytical chemist at Pfizer, "Triacylated lipoprotein are nasty. They cause the 'cytokine storm' and then immunosuppression also known as POST-SEPSIS syndrome. They feck up your B cell germinal centers, and render you incompetent to viral infections."[101]

This sounds like the same thing our dead holistic doctors were trying to say? Hmm…looks like the same mechanisms are at work

99   Eichenwald, Kurt. "Killer Pharmacy: Inside a Medical Mass Murder Case." *Newsweek*. 20 Sept. 2016. Web. <http://www.newsweek.com/2015/04/24/inside-one-most-murderous-corpo-rate-crimes-us-history-322665.html>

100 *Centers for Disease Control and Prevention*. Centers for Disease Control and Prevention, 18 Feb. 2016. Web. <https://www.cdc.gov/hai/outbreaks/meningitis-map-large.html>

101 "VACCINES BUSTED." *Vimeo*. 15 Jan. 2017. Web. <https://vimeo.com/180644386>

here. Toxins are added to vaccines to stealth-bomb your immune system. This allows any dormant virus, like herpes or Epstein-Barr, free attacks on your body and brain, along with any other virus being injected via the vaccine.

So, this is why thimerosal was used in the vaccines to prevent LYMErix or post-sepsis outcome, this fungal-viral synergy, which causes chronic fatigue, cancer, Lyme, AIDS, autism, and other immunosuppressive diseases. They knew that vials could become tainted with a fungal-like antigen; that is why they added thimerosal to vaccines. Regardless, if your child is immunosuppressed via a cold, living in a moldy home, not knowing they have Lyme or any other immunosuppressive disease, the virus becomes activated in them, even if it had thimerosal in it. Yes, the virus or disease that the vaccine was to prevent, which makes it NOT a vaccine at all! This is why children are getting brain damage from MMR vaccine. Measles, Mumps, and Rubella are brain-tropic viruses, and they get to attack your child's brain and nervous system when your child's doctor plays Russian roulette with your child's government-mandatory vaccines.

Whistleblower Kathleen Dickson

If this doesn't have the makings for a movie like *The Fugitive*, starring Harrison Ford as Dr. Richard Kimble, Tommy Lee Jones as Marshal Samuel Gerard, and Andrew Davis as Dr. Charles Nichols, nothing will. Remember when Dr. Kimble discovered the pharmaceutical company Devlin MacGregor was falsifying their findings on their new drug called Provasic? Through his investigation, Dr. Kimble discovered that it caused liver damage, which would prevent it from getting FDA approval.

The story goes on to where Dr. Nichols, a so-called friend, was being paid by the drug company to hide the report. Dr. Kimble was going to put a stop to this new dangerous drug when they set him up for killing his wife. The plot goes on to Dr. Kimble escaping the authorities via a train wreck and becoming a fugitive.

Marshal Gerard was hired to track Dr. Kimble and bring him into custody. The plot thickens to where Dr. Kimble was able to prove to the world that he was set up and that the drug was not any good.

This story reminds me of my friend and whistleblower Kathleen Dickson, who is the scientist that discovered the crime. She questioned the FDA, CDC and all of the "Powers that Be" on the fake LYMErix vaccine, a vaccine that is supposed to protect you from the disease, not give you the disease. She also showed how other vaccines are causing "LYMErix" disease, or POST-SEPSIS.

She filed a RICO (Racketeering Influenced and Corrupt Organization Act) Complaint in 2003, asking the FDA to do their job and prosecute the criminals.

Kathleen is like Dr. Kimble in *The Fugitive*, who was falsely accused and thrown in jail. Kathleen's children were taken away from her because she was trying to expose the truth. They charged her with neglecting her children with Lyme disease because she was too busy emailing and faxing government officials the truth about Lyme disease. She was pointing out how the scientific community was covering up the truth about Lyme and how her children could not get treatments or help.

Hard to believe they could say she was medically neglecting her children! No one gets treatments when they have Lyme disease. There is medically nothing they can give you to help you get better and the "Powers that Be" know this and are allowing people with Lyme to be ridiculed, suffer and die!

Thanks to real science and the internet, this crime against humanity is finally being exposed. Kathleen is still a huge Lyme activist and isn't backing down or staying quiet. Kathleen and all of us in the Lyme community want validation, vindication, and prosecution of these Lyme criminals. Unfortunately, the "Powers that Be" are keeping the government from doing their job. We are still waiting for a Senate hearing to force the justice department to hear and try the case that Attorney General Richard Blumenthal brought to them in a civil suit he filed when he was Connecticut Attorney General in 2006. The case shows the antitrust investigation that uncovered serious flaws in the Infectious Diseases Society of America's (IDSA) process for writing its 2006 Lyme disease guidelines, and the IDSA said they would agree to reassess the guidelines with an entity that doesn't have anything to gain.

Blumenthal's findings include the following:

- The IDSA failed to conduct a conflicts of interest review for any of the panelists prior to their appointment to the 2006 Lyme disease guideline panel;
- Subsequent disclosures demonstrate that several of the 2006 Lyme disease panelists had conflicts of interest;
- The IDSA failed to follow its own procedures for appointing the 2006 panel chairman and members, enabling the chairman, who held a bias regarding the existence of chronic Lyme, to handpick a like-minded panel without scrutiny by or formal approval of the IDSA's oversight committee;

- The IDSA's 2000 and 2006 Lyme disease panels refused to accept or meaningfully consider information regarding the existence of chronic Lyme disease, once removing a panelist from the 2000 panel who dissented from the group's position on chronic Lyme disease to achieve "consensus";
- The IDSA blocked appointment of scientists and physicians with divergent views on chronic Lyme who sought to serve on the 2006 guidelines panel by informing them that the panel was fully staffed, even though it was later expanded;
- The IDSA portrayed another medical association's Lyme disease guidelines as corroborating its own when it knew that the two panels shared several authors, including the chairmen of both groups, and were working on guidelines at the same time. In allowing its panelists to serve on both groups at the same time, IDSA violated its own conflicts of interest policy.[102]

Have you connected the dots yet? This is all pretty scary, but don't lose hope! Get your copy of my *Life Healing Handbook* at **www.OvercomingLymeDisease.com/free-handbook** to learn more about resources you can use to protect yourself and improve your health.

---

[102] General, Office of the Attorney. "Attorney General: Attorney General's Investigation Reveals Flawed Lyme Disease Guideline Process, IDSA Agrees to Reassess Guidelines, Install Independent Arbiter." *Attorney General: Attorney General's Investigation Reveals Flawed Lyme Disease Guideline Process, IDSA Agrees To Reassess Guidelines, Install Independent Arbiter.* Web. <http://www.ct.gov/AG/cwp/view.asp?a=2795&q=414284>

CHAPTER 11

The Dangers of Root Canals, Mercury Fillings, and the Use of Fluoride

"I'm not gonna give up, shut up, or let up, until I'm taken up…
as a matter of fact, I'm just getting warmed up."
–Zig Ziglar

March 2013, I mysteriously fell ill after a routine dental cleaning. My dentist told me the crown on my root canal tooth needed to be replaced. The dentist fitted me for a new one and put a temporary crown on. Within a day or two, I was unable to function normally and was in constant pain. I didn't realize the dental appointment and mystery illness were because of the infection leaking into my body from the dead tooth.

Root canals are the only medical procedure where they leave a dead body part in you. These dead teeth are the perfect host for infection (viral, bacterial, fungal or parasitic) to grow and spread. Taking an antibiotic or using herbs that heal are useless when trying to fully eradicate the infection because there is no blood supply to the necrotic (dead/infected) tissue. This makes having a root canal the perfect breeding ground for any "Superbug." You will continue to have an infection as long as you have a place to harvest it, hence it is my belief that you should have your root canal surgically removed, by a knowledgeable biological dentist.

No matter what you may hear, there is no way for a doctor to guarantee you that root canals are 100% safe, especially with your new awareness of the real case definition of Lyme or Post-Sepsis Syndrome.

Knowledge is power! My retired holistic doctor, Rich Easterling, begged me NOT to have any root canals done eighteen years prior to my "diagnosis" of Lyme disease! He tried to explain to me why, but I didn't grasp the information and when I questioned my dentist and endodontist, they laughed and informed me that they were safe. Instead of trusting in Dr. Easterling's knowledge, I gave into our brainwashed, "God-like" faith in MDs and DDSs and had the root canal done.

Tooth decay happens, and at times we can develop an abscessed tooth. According to my extremely knowledgeable biological dentist, Natalie Horn DD.S, "An abscessed tooth is infection draining into the bloodstream and affecting the heart." Depending on the tooth's location, it also affects the organs or body parts that it is connected to.

There is so much evidence out there that proves root canals are not as safe as once thought. With the rise in these "Superbugs" that don't respond to antibiotics or Western medicine, it makes total sense to be proactive with your health and not have a root canal done if your tooth goes bad. It is far healthier for you to have it pulled by a biological dentist who knows how to safely clean out the infection in the socket of the tooth and the surrounding jaw bone and ligaments.

All dentists should be aware of spirochetes that hang out in the mouth that lower immune response and cause chronic diseases. Check out what *The Journal of Dental Research* says about how Oral Spirochete Treponema denticola causes periodontal disease and more:

> There is compelling evidence that treponemes are involved in the etiology of several chronic diseases, including chronic periodontitis as well as other forms of periodontal disease. There are interesting parallels with other chronic diseases caused by treponemes that may indicate similar virulence characteristics. Chronic periodontitis is a polymicrobial disease, and recent animal studies indicate that co-infection of *Treponema denticola* with other periodontal pathogens can enhance alveolar bone resorption. The bacterium has a suite of molecular determinants that could enable it to cause tissue damage and subvert the host immune response. In addition to this, it has several non-classic virulence determinants that enable it to interact with other pathogenic bacteria and the host in ways that are likely to promote disease progression.[103]

Having all four of my infected root canals removed was another big part of my journey to heal. I went through two dentists and one endodontist before I found Dr. Natalie Horn. The other dentist and endodontist said I needed to redo all of my root canals, except one that was severely abscessed in my lower right jaw bone. They said that the abscessed root canal needed to be surgically removed and prepped for an implant. They also thought that I was going to lose the baby tooth that was next to the root canal due to the infection.

[103]   Dashper, S.G., C.A. Seers, K.H. Tan, and E.C. Reynolds. "Virulence Factors of the Oral Spirochete *Treponema Denticola." Journal of Dental Research*. SAGE Publications, June 2011. Web. <https://www.ncbi.nlm.nih.gov/pmc/articles/PMC3144123/>

What these doctors don't understand is that Lyme and their co-infections will continue to thrive in these dead spaces, regardless of what they do. After questioning their knowledge, I fired them and hired Dr. Horn.

The infection was so severe in my abscessed area that I lost a lot of bone, which made it risky for an implant. By the time I had my first root canal taken out, I could hardly open my mouth without sheer pain. Good thing I was already on a liquid diet, as I could not chew my food. Dr. Horn is such an amazing dentist, not only was she able to surgically remove the infected root canal and stop my pain, she was able to save my baby tooth too.

What Are Your Options When Your Teeth Go Bad?

Dr. Natalie Horn shares this valuable information:

One question that is frequently asked with discussion of a crown is: Do I need a root canal before it? Due to insult to the tooth (whether repetitive cavities, fillings or initial fracture) it is believed that the irritation can cause a nerve to be irritated enough to fail. Research has changed the early belief of RCT (root canal) prior to every crown, to only as needed. Technology has allowed instruments to go through crowns and the ability to look into canals with high powered microscopes and find all canals. Thus, due to the expense and refined technology of this profession our office does refer to a very highly qualified team of endodontists. With that being said, comes the controversy of to have a root canal or not? At this time in technology, the controversy has been raised on the latest finding of an autoimmune response with materials used in RCT's along with lingering bacteria that is unable to be removed from the structure of the tooth.

The conversation that comes up is bearing on a much bigger picture. What options are available if the abscessed tooth is removed?

Depending on the patient's view and values, a root canal can achieve an immediate need to save a tooth. Most teeth must be replaced to establish stability of the remaining teeth and bite.

Options if tooth is removed:

- Removal partial
  a. Pros - Cost effective
  b. Cons - Food can get under it during eating. Clasps on adjacent teeth can trap food and increase caries (cavity) risk
- Bridge
  a. Pros - Cost effective
  b. Cons - Adjacent teeth must be prepared as a crown- Unable to floss like regular teeth. Need to thread under bridge thus increased risk of recurrent cavities under bridge pontic region.
- Implant
  a. Pros - Unable to get cavity, Easy to floss and longevity
  b. Cons - Amount of time for final crown- approx. six months- expense and need for additional bone graft.

Huge big red flag here! "Technology has allowed instruments to go through crowns and the ability to look into canals with high powered microscopes and find all canals." Dentists and endodontists can now see that root canals don't work and harvest bacteria. Sort of like how we can now see and have scientific proof that there was a Big Bang in the creation of the universe by using high power telescopes, the Hubble and NASA's Spitzer Space Telescope.[104]

Mercury Fillings Are Toxic to Our Bodies

Root canals are not the only dangerous dental procedure we have done. Mercury/silver fillings are extremely toxic and detrimental to our health. Think about it: mercury fillings in our mouths are toxic before they go into our mouths and then after they are taken out. It is crazy that we are being told, or brainwashed, that they are not toxic while they are in our mouths.

How To Safely Remove Mercury Fillings

Here is some additional information from Dr. Horn on how they remove mercury fillings:

> Cavity removal with filling replacement can be accomplished with multiple choices. Our practice no longer gives the option of Amalgams (silver fillings) due to the high controversy of the mercury component. With removal of amalgams, we take all precautions to minimize contamination.

1. Oxygen placement
2. Rubber dam

---

[104] *NASA.* NASA. Web.
https://www.nasa.gov/feature/goddard/2016/hubble-team-breaks-cosmic-distance-record

3. Heavy water and evacuation
4. Minimal to no touch of the amalgam filling (outlined) upon removal.

Replacement options:
- Resin composite (white)
- Inlays or onlays (porcelain)
- Crown material optional depending on personal choice.
  a. Porcelain
  b. Porcelain fused to high noble metal (stabile)
  c. Gold-anti-cavity properties

For more information, go to http://www.nataliehorndds.com

By the way, the so-called biological dentist (not Dr. Horn) that took out my last mercury fillings did not use the rubber dam and my hair tissue mineral analysis now says I have more mercury in my body. Time for another deep tissue cleanse!

The Dangers of Fluoride

Let's see what the ADA (American Dental Association) and the CDC have to say about fluoride:

> Sixty years ago, Grand Rapids, Michigan became the world's 1st city to adjust the level of fluoride in its water supply. Since that time, fluoridation has dramatically improved the oral health of tens of millions of Americans. Community water fluoridation is the single most effective public health measure to prevent tooth decay. Additionally, the Centers for Disease Control and

Prevention proclaimed community water fluoridation as one of 10 great public health achievements of the 20th century.[105]

Imagine that, the CDC says that water fluoridation is one of the top ten public health achievements of the twentieth century. Let's look into this a little further, shall we? In the article "The Dangers of Fluoride and Fluoridation," Schachter MD, F.A.C.A.M. writes:

> In addition to the well documented toxic effects of fluoride, fluoride even at dosages of 1 part per million, found in artificially fluoridated water, can inhibit enzyme systems, damage the immune system, contribute to calcification of soft tissues, worsen arthritis and, of course, cause dental fluorosis in children. These are unsightly white, yellow or brown spots that are found in teeth exposed to fluoride during childhood. In 1993, the Subcommittee on Health Effects of Ingested Fluoride of the National Research Council admitted that 8% to 51% and sometimes up to 80% of the children living in fluoridated areas have dental fluorosis. Malnourished people, particularly children, usually targeted for fluoridation, are at greater risks to experience fluoride's harmful effects.[106]

Did you notice it "can inhibit enzyme systems, damage the immune system, contribute to calcification of soft tissues, worsen arthritis"? Sounds cancer-causing to me.

You can make your own healthy toothpaste by mixing organic coconut oil, baking soda, and peppermint oil. I like to mix up my routine by using this recipe some days and using Real Purity's

---

[105] http://www.ada.org/~/media/ADA/Member%20Center/FIles/fluoridation_facts.ashx

[106] "The Dangers of Fluoride and Fluoridation." *The Dangers of Fluoride and Fluoridation.* Web. <http://www.mbschachter.com/dangers_of_fluoride_and_fluorida.htm>

cinnamon toothpaste on other days. For even better cleaning, gargle with food-grade hydrogen peroxide. By the way, hydrogen peroxide is what all good dentists and endodontists recommend when there is an infection in the mouth. Hmm, I guess they know it helps against spirochetes and their infections?

To learn more healthy, alternative recipes and beneficial uses of hydrogen peroxide, go to my *Life Healing Handbook* at **www.OvercomingLymeDisease.com/free-handbook**.

PART THREE

Advanced Strategies

CHAPTER 12

The Crucial Role of Enzymes

"You don't know what you don't know,
until you know what you don't know, you know?"
–George Koffeman

Did you know that every organ and system in our body uses enzymes to run it? True! Our creator made it that way. That is why having a diet of fresh organic raw fruits and vegetables is crucial for a healthy body!

Cooking destroys enzymes, therefore, raw is best. Of course, we live in a society where eating a raw organic diet is almost impossible. That is why taking enzymes should be a part of our everyday life!

As I look back in my journey of healing, I can see how when I took my enzymes on a daily basis, before, after, and in between every meal, I had energy and could eat almost anything I wanted to! Unfortunately, I thought once I had arrived at feeling well, I could stop taking my enzymes. I was wrong!

Three years ago, before I fell deathly ill, I had stopped taking my enzymes. Why? Excellent question, since I felt myself slowly getting sick! I now know that it is because I didn't truly understand the importance of them in my everyday life. Knowledge is power!

Knowing why and truly comprehending why you are doing something keeps you on target.

Via information my holistic Dr. Richard Easterling would gather on me either through a twenty-four hour urine analysis, blood work, iridology, applied kinesiology, or a hair tissue mineral analysis, he was able to determine what nutrients my body was lacking and needed more of.

Food Digestion Is the Top Priority of Our Body's Internal System

In the book *The Truth About Cancer*'s bonus PDF "Enzymes Explained," Ty Bollinger reports, "that enzymes are more important than the air you breathe, the water you drink, and the food you eat."[107] He goes on to say:

> Without enzymes you wouldn't be able to breathe, swallow, drink, eat, think, see, or digest food. All of your cells, organs, bones, muscles, and tissues are run by enzymes. Your immune system, kidneys, pancreas, liver, spleen, and the blood stream depend on enzymes...

> The more we depend on our body to create digestive enzymes, the more stress we put on our body and less time the body's systems and organs have for rebuilding and replacing worn out and damaged cells and tissue and keeping the immune system strong.

---

[107] Bollinger, Ty M. *The Truth about Cancer: What You Need to Know about Cancer's History, Treatment, and Prevention.* Carlsbad, CA: Hay House, 2016. Print.

With this knowledge, I hope we all seek and use enzymes for our body on a daily basis to either regain our health or to live a healthy life that our creator planned for us to live!

Let's look at what Kathleen Dickson, the whistleblower of fake LYMErix vaccine, says about why you are sick in her video "Validating Your Illness," shall we? Kathleen says that Lyme patients have:

> Post-traumatic stress disorder, organ damage, dealing with multiple infections, chronic fatigue infections of all kinds, herpes virus and mycoplasma...

> You have gut problems, gut leakage, you eat something, you go into a food coma. With post-sepsis, you have a deregulation of your immune cells in your gut, you are not metabolizing food appropriately and all of those toxins are getting into your bloodstream, so of course you are tired an hour after you eat. Same as the blood/brain barrier, it is also affected and now it is loose. All kinds of things that wouldn't get in there would. So you are very sick.[108]

She is totally right. I couldn't say it any better!

Dr. Easterling can help you understand the mechanisms at work here. Let's see what Dr. Easterling says about these chronic infections and the blood–brain barrier in his report "PROTEIN-PROTEASE-DEFICIENCY and HYDROCHLORIC ACID."

> Protein deficiency implies a deficiency in protease. A protein deficiency compromises the immune alliance, leaving a person susceptible to frequent or chronic infections, either bacterial –

---

[108]   "Fireside Chat Chapter 1." *Vimeo.* 10 Jan. 2017. Web. <https://vimeo.com/191399290>

or viral – or both. It can make them vulnerable to other more serious conditions, including cancer.

Protease deficiency can lead to edema (retention of fluid). The edema can manifest itself in various places in the body, including swelling of the hands and feet as well as fluid in the ears. When a buildup of toxins in the large intestine happens, toxic colon syndrome can occur. This is another condition that results from a protease deficiency that in turn, can lead to various intestinal problems including chronic constipation, appendicitis and even cancer of the colon. Toxic colon syndrome is not to be confused with Ileocecal Valve Syndrome, which is another matter altogether.

Over half of the protein digested is converted to glucose. This follows therefore, that a protease deficiency thus a protein deficiency, can lead to and be directly involved with, hypoglycemia (low blood sugar), and its accompanying symptoms such as moodiness, depression, irritability and exhaustion.

Protein, when digested properly, supplies acidity to the blood. When protein is not digested, the blood acquires excess alkaline reserves which must be continuously dumped via the kidneys into the urine. When there is such an alkaline reserve, it can result in anxiety. This can be to such a degree that these conditions are often treated with prescription tranquilizers. These drugs do absolutely nothing to address the underlying imbalance and the symptom chase and suppression dance is underway. There is another phenomenon that accompanies this situation.

Since the very important mineral calcium is carried by the blood partly bound to digested protein and partly in ionic (salt) form, protease deficiency and inadequate protein digestion along with the resulting excess alkaline reserves can lead to calcium metabolism problems. These problems include osteoporosis, osteoarthritis, degenerative disk problems and bone spurs. A further role that protease plays is in the prevention and elimination of blood clots.

Protease is necessary to digest protein; Protease digests protein into smaller units called amino acids. Remember that not only is there protein from food but also from other organisms that are composed of protein, such as the coating on certain viruses, toxins from dead bacteria as well as other micro-organisms, and certain other harmful substances produced at sites of injury and /or inflammation.

Amino acids are the building blocks of the 40,000 different proteins in the body. This includes enzymes, hormones and the key brain chemical messenger molecules called neurotransmitters. Eight of the amino acids cannot be made by the body. These amino acids are called essential, while other amino acids that can be synthesized by the body are termed non-essential. I do not agree with this classification since the so called non-essential amino acids are in fact very essential for life but under proper circumstances can be manufactured by the body if the essential ones are present. Such proper circumstances may not be present during times of various stresses, malnutrition, illness, protease/protein deficiency and any number of other common occurrences in life.

For a quick understanding of the biochemistry involved, it is important to realize the extent to which protease deficiency and protein digestion and protein deficiency are involved. Protein deficiencies are more common than not and protein digestion is not necessarily automatic or average. Add to this the fact that many people have low or no protein/ high carbohydrate diets and there are added dimensions to the problem. As for the biochemistry, the human body is made up of water, minerals, protein, fat carbohydrates, vitamins and enzymes. Water is essential in maintaining the fluidity of the various elements or ingredients found in the bloodstream. Water enters into many metabolic functions and reactions. Minerals are a part of every cell but most of the time in a reactive way, such as a part of an enzyme. Vitamins are a part of the enzyme system and are catalystic in many reactions.

Fat gives insulation and acts as a reserve supply of energy. Energy is normally supplied by carbohydrates. Protein is the substance of which every cell is made and without it, the other elements or ingredients could not function properly. Protein, in the absence of water in the cells, would account for nearly 75% of the dry weight of the cells.

Protein, as we know, is made up of amino acids which have been characterized as essential and nonessential. In so describing, science must assume average and automatic digestion in humans. Average and automatic digestion is not found in most humans in the civilized world.

There have been numerous diets and trends to ignore or downgrade the need for protein in the diet. Carbohydrates have been in vogue and "carbohydrate loading" popular with numerous athletes. This may have come about partly by the establishment of the SAD statistics. Many Standard American Diets (SAD) are too high in protein (especially certain types or sources), and too low in vegetables and fruits. However protein in the diet and the digestion, assimilation, absorption etc., are too often overlooked in today's pseudo-scientific approach to diet and nutrition.

There are a number of established facts that should be an indication of just how important protein consumption and digestion is when it comes to health and wellness:

- Every second the bone marrow, crucial to the immune alliance, makes 2,500,000 red blood cells.
- Blood platelets, the disk shaped structures in the blood whose functions relate to the arrest of bleeding and in blood coagulation (homeostasis), are replaced every four days. This means that about 500,000,000 platelets are replaced every day.
- The entire mucosal lining of the intestinal tract turns over or regenerates every 14 days.
- All the white blood cells are replaced every ten.
- The outer skin, often called the third kidney, is replaced about every twenty.

What do these, as well as many of the bodily functions and processes have in common?

Each and every one of these functions and regenerating processes require amino acids, which require protein consumption and digestion. All of the carbohydrates, fats, vitamins and minerals in the world cannot make these functions and processes happen without protein and proper protein digestion and assimilation, etc. Newborn babies have the highest protein requirement and need approximately 35% of their daily diet as protein for optimal growth and development.

There are approximately 40 amino acids known and identified at this time and some of them have very definite characteristic actions which can be of great benefit in maintaining and restoring health in a number of special ways. Some ways that have been proven to be useful and effective:

- Immune function stimulation and support
- Supporting and assisting detoxification
- Lowering cholesterol and triglyceride levels
- Harmlessly and reasonably reducing appetite
- Increasing appetite when necessary such as in anorexia
- Reducing blood pressure
- Helping to fight addiction

Without doubt, protein consumption, digestion, assimilation, absorption etc., are critical to health and wellness. Some of the amino acids are extremely important in the process of normal nerve transmission and have to pass the blood brain barrier, a very selective barrier. The desired effect is best accomplished by the proper consumption and digestion of protein. When therapeutic supplementation is undertaken, in order to pass the very selective blood brain barrier, the amino acid supplements are best taken alone on an empty stomach. The reason for this is that when all the amino acids are present they have a tendency to compete for a gateway into the brain. An example is the amino acid phenylalanine taken with food for depression. Taken that way, phenylalanine would most probably be totally ineffective, but taken alone on an empty stomach an hour before a meal could prove to be phenomenal. Space and time do not permit discussing all the benefits and therapeutic usage of individual amino acids or the absolute necessity of amino acids in life that comes from proper protein consumption and digestion.

One of the more often overlooked facets of protein digestion/consumption is involved with blood sugar levels. The storage of glucose, as well as the transportation of glucose, is very much dependent on this process that is taken for granted more times than not. When it is questioned, it usually is because someone is thought to be" getting older" and things are a little off because of aging. Then hydrochloric acid is recommended because the patient does not have enough, or maybe there is too much, and an HCL blocker is used, and of course, if one drug or "medicine" is used, others are sure to follow. The indigestion/ antacid industry has become so large that conventional medicine, never one to miss out on possible revenues, has come up with a disease, Acid Reflux Disease. This disease has been "discovered" along with many, many others, because of the obvious Cartel connections and the fact that the technicians dispensing the drugs have too much calculus and far too little biochemistry. As for how this connects to blood sugar levels, protein digestion or a lack thereof plays a significant role in a number of related physical, mental and emotional conditions and their accompanying signs and symptoms.

There are times patients come to our clinic after being diagnosed with numerous disorders and conditions, both physical and mental. Often the doctors can find nothing wrong with them and after a ride on the "insurance freeway" and any number of "approved" and costly tests, the traffic is directed to another insurance freeway called the "specialist". If this proves to be unproductive (for the patient, as it is a lock for the doctors, drug and insurance companies), being productive and extremely profitable as far as they are concerned. Then many times the last insurance approved route is the psychiatric one. This in turn, leads to drugs and more drugs, therapies, group therapies, and perhaps even a little electro-shock "therapy". Patently done and occurring time after time is the total disregard and overlooking of any directly related physical/nutritional beginning causes of these "mental and emotional" conditions.

If abnormal brain chemistry and activity are concluding factors in diagnosing mental illness, then in a sane world one would look to abnormal body chemistry that could be caused by nutritional imbalances. The very imbalance in the body's own biochemistry leads to not only nutritional problems, but hormonal imbalance and abnormal brain chemistry. These problems, not limited to but including protein/protease deficiency, sugar reactiveness and intolerance (the inability to digest disaccharides into simple sugars), and thyroid disorders especially hypothyroidism (an underactive thyroid gland), as well as pituitary and other endocrine considerations have commonalities and overlapping symptoms.

In discussing protein and the life processes involved, keep in mind that those who are deficient in protease cannot digest proteins properly. Some people become vegetarians and still have difficulty digesting plant protein and when diagnosed by a qualified and competent enzyme therapist, the deficiencies become obvious and treatable. When left untreated, a digestive enzyme deficiency can lead to metabolic deficiencies, as the body tries to maintain homeostatic balance, and will rob from one system to pay another in the quest for homeostasis. The protease deficiency that can lead to the accumulation of alkaline reserves results in a tendency toward alkalinity and an alkaline pH in the urine. This excess of alkaline reserves comes about because there is not enough digested protein to supply the necessary acidity. In order to supply acidity (hydrochloric acid) to the stomach needed in the process of digestion, there has to be the necessary acidity in the blood in order to donate it to the digestion. Some common symptoms of an over alkaline system are frequent sighing, anxiety and even full blown "panic attacks", among others. Protein is a carrier and along with the protein/protease deficiency and the excess alkaline reserves in the bloodstream, there is a lack of calcium being properly transported. This is another factor in anxiety and an inability to relax. Sugar reactiveness and intolerance is another factor in many problems both physical and mental/emotional. Some of these symptoms and conditions that are directly caused by sugar intolerance/reactiveness include: autism, attention deficit disorder (ADD), hyperactive attention disorder, overly aggressive behavior, depression, irritability, bipolar and schizophrenic disorders, insomnia, nightmares and panic attacks. Some of the extreme symptoms are seen in people that are sugar intolerant/ sugar reactive, vitamin B deficient, and hypothyroid which is intricately involved with hypoglycemia, commonly called low blood sugar (low blood glucose). Glucose is formed in the body from the digestion of protein, carbohydrates, sugars and B-complex vitamins. It is required in brain activity and nutrition. When there is inadequate glucose arriving in the brain the apple cart starts to tip and problems result. The cause of all this is seen in three primary factors directly involved in the prevention of the glucose arriving in the brain efficiently. The first is the inability to digest sugar. Secondly is inadequate protein digestion, as over half the digested protein is eventually converted to glucose and protein is necessary to carry and store glucose. A third factor is the B-vitamin deficiency as B vitamins are required in the transportation of sugar (glucose) to the brain.

A large number of Americans are sugar reactive/sugar intolerant to varying extents.

Refined carbohydrate consumption in America is very high and the number of unhealthy people has been on the rise. The overeating of refined sugar and an inability to digest it is evident in many so-called health problems including allergies and asthma. This may be due to a deficiency in disaccharides (the enzymes that digest sugars: lactase, sucrase, maltase). This digestion occurs primarily in the small intestine. When sugars are ingested beyond an individual's own digestive capacity and their ability to process it, numerous problems occur. The refined bleached sugars and starches (rice and flour) are rendered ineffective for good nutrition and are void of B vitamins needed to transport glucose into the brain. Because of this situation even those who seem to tolerate and be able to digest sugars are still unable to utilize them effectively because of the inability to transport the glucose properly.

Another factor mentioned earlier that affects so many people is hypothyroidism. (See earlier work on thyroid). There are many factors involved in the thyroid and the entire endocrine system that are not considered in conventional medicine and that are significant in the biochemistry of living beings. Hypothyroidism is linked closely to some forms of depression and numerous symptoms of mental illness. It is also linked to many digestive problems including poor blood profiles, high cholesterol/triglyceride levels, hypoglycemia etc.. The sugar intolerant, hypothyroid, low blood sugar people have common and similar sounding symptoms that are all too often chased. Chasing symptoms is common and has the ability, like drugs, to mask the real problem and give varying degrees of relief. Many so-called "natural practitioners" when treating a problem, take a medical diagnosis, assume it is correct, and treat this "condition" with so-called "nutrition" and more "natural band-aids" without considering digestive ability and nutritional deficiency based upon solid, provable and repeatable evidence, that when done competently, should dovetail with other sensible prognostic and diagnostic disciplines.

The use of actual nutrition with a good diet based upon solid evidence concerning digestion, absorption assimilation and elimination, cannot be over emphasized. While the use of a specific, possibly life-saving medical procedure or drug done necessarily and competently is not disputed, the overly heroic procedures and the irresponsible overprescribing of harmful drugs inappropriately called "medicines" certainly should be. Many times drugs not only do not help people but often make them worse and give them new problems. The people in this country, as well as other countries, are used and abused by the drug "cartel" and its pushers or technicians (doctors and pharmacists) whose knowledge of actual nutrition and biochemistry is usually non-existent. Doctor to many means teacher. In this country the average allopathic "doctor", the visible link with the "cartel" (made up of the medical schools, researchers, and pharmaceutical companies, all aligned with the so called "insurance companies"), do not have the time to shake hands with or even listen to their patients, let alone teach them anything. This incredible worldwide network that makes up the misnamed system of "health care", is without doubt the "ultimate monopoly", with vast numbers of corporations and individuals involved with making a living from other people trying to live, with greed and profit as their bottom line.

The use of nutrition, especially using plant enzymes in digestion, assimilation, absorption and elimination, with other good prognostic and diagnostic tools to help people be healthy and well, would go far in making this a healthier, happier and better place.[109]

Wow! What an amazing description of how protein digestion and protease enzymes are important to everyone's health! Dr.

---

[109] "Protein-Protease Deficiency and Hydrochloric Acid." *Real Purity Blog.* 17 Jan. 2017. Web. <http://www.realpurity.com/blog/protein-protease-deficiency-hydrochloric-acid/>

Easterling, at one point, was one of the top sellers of these life-giving enzymes. He helped many cancer patients live longer, healthier lives when they followed his protocols, including enzymes, and stayed on an organic diet. This is even after they were cut, burned, poisoned and left for dead by the medical establishment.

Get your copy of my *Life Healing Handbook* at
www.OvercomingLymeDisease.com/free-handbook
to learn more about enzymes and diet tips
from the experts I've consulted.

CHAPTER 13

Food Allergies
and Chiropractic Care

"Your old patterns may be strong but YOU are stronger the moment you MAKE YOUR DECISION."

–Mary Morrissey

August 2014, I became bedridden and unable to eat or drink anything. All of the healthy foods and drinks I had been consuming became like poison to my body. As soon as I tried to consume it, I vomited. I now know that I was not rotating my foods or diet. I was eating the same thing every day, thinking it was good for me. Instead, I developed allergic reactions to it.

Dr. Coller, at the Born Clinic, ran a food allergy test on me during my first office visit with him. The results: everything I was eating I had now become allergic to. This test was backed up with my Hair Tissue Mineral Analysis that showed what foods I should be eating and what ones not to eat.

I stayed away from the offending foods until I was done with having all of my root canals removed and finished my IV oxygen treatments. I went from a strict diet of juicing, herbal teas, and eating organic, unprocessed foods that these offending foods weren't a part of, to adding them into my diet.

When I went to California in January of 2015 for Silpada's Leadership Conference, I started eating and drinking whatever I wanted. During this time, I started to feel sick again. Mind you, I wasn't on my special enzyme formula yet, and I had stopped taking my Endo-met supplements from ARL labs because I had run out of them during my long stay in CA.

Since I still had no place to live as I was going through my divorce, my beautiful Aunt Christina and her husband Jason took me in. They were a huge support to me as I was grieving the loss of my marriage and broken family. I was also still healing from the horrific experiences I had while dealing with the medical establishment as I healed my body from Lyme disease.

My Uncle Jason's parents, Sarah and Russ, lived a few blocks away and were extremely supportive and generous with their time and resources with me. I begin trying to work out with Jason's awesome dad, Russ. I was walking three miles a day and started to lift weights. After the first weight lifting workout, I was in extreme pain in my back. Since I was in California and didn't know whom to call, I Googled applied kinesiology doctors in the area. The first doctor I called never returned my call, which was very unfortunate for him, but lucky for me. The second answered right away. His name is Dr. Benn Rocco.

Talk about a jackpot! Dr. Rocco knew and studied the teachings of Dr. Bernard Jensen and Dr. George Goodheart, like Dr. Easterling. Dr. Rocco really focused on Dr. Walter Schmidt's protocol on treating food allergies. Dr. Schmidt was one of the founding fathers of International College of Applied Kinesiology, along with Dr. George Koffeman and Dr. Goodheart.

Not All Chiropractors Are Created Equal

Dr. Rocco is not just a chiropractor. He is a Chiropractor of Applied Kinesiology and Chiropractic Neurology. There are not too many chiropractors that have his credentials. Dr. Benn is old school and takes his time educating his patients on diet, nutritional supplementation, and exercise. Not only that, but before he will adjust you, he has you lay down on a table with a warm wet heat pack on your back and one wrapped around your neck to help relax your muscles so he can give you a proper adjustment.

During my hour and a half consultation with Dr. Rocco, he adjusted me, did some muscle testing, took my body temperature and blood pressure, and did a saliva test to see if my pH was balanced. To my surprise, I had a fever. I couldn't remember the last time I had had one. My blood pressure was good, but my pH was a low 6.

That is when he asked me about my diet and asked if I would be diligent in doing a 21-Day Food Elimination Diet, and allow him to do muscle testing for nutritional deficiencies. Of course, I said yes; I wanted to get better. So, he started me on his program.

The enzymes, probiotics, and other supplements for my body that Dr. Rocco tested me for and put me on were the same type of nutrients I was on via the hair analysis and suggested by Dr. Easterling. Yes, I think Dr. Rocco knew what he was doing with me and that there must be some accuracy with using applied kinesiology for your nutritional needs. The trick is finding a knowledgeable doctor that is good at it. Just like any other medical doctor, not all doctors are created equal.

Tequila: the Only Upper Alcohol

When I went in for another appointment with Dr. Rocco, I asked if there was any alcohol I could drink. That is when I learned a very important lesson—tequila! It is the only upper alcohol there is. It helps lower blood sugar[110], it contains no yeast or extra sugar, it helps with digestion, and it fights cholesterol.[111]

So, during this difficult time, I got to have a cocktail. I would fresh squeeze two clementines and one lime in tequila on the rocks. It is one of my favorite drinks, go figure!

How Food Allergies Affect You

Dr. Rocco writes:

> Food Allergies result in nutritional deficiencies which lead to metabolic imbalance, immune system compromise, and the appearance of symptoms. At this point there's a choice. You can go to an MD, get a medical diagnosis, have your symptoms named, get prescription drugs, experience disappointment and failure, and even risk potentially severe side effects. Or you can address the Food Allergies and resolve the primary, underlying cause of your symptoms safely, naturally, and without the risk of potentially harmful drugs.

---

[110] "Tequila Plant Is Possible Sweetener for Diabetics-helps Reduce Blood Sugar, Weight." *Phys. org - News and Articles on Science and Technology*. Web. <https://phys.org/news/2014-03-tequila-sweetener-diabeticshelps-blood-sugar.html>

[111] "Effects of Different Sources of Fructans on Body Weight, Blood Metabolites and Fecal Bacteria in Normal and Obese Non-diabetic and Diabetic Rats." *Plant Foods for Human Nutrition (Dordrecht, Netherlands)*. U.S. National Library of Medicine. Web. <https://www.ncbi.nlm.nih.gov/pubmed/22210166>

What do Fibromyalgia, Chronic Fatigue Syndrome, Arthritis, Asthma, Migraine, Gout, Depression, ADD/ADHD, IBS, and Obesity, as well as a whole host of common and uncommon maladies including the entire list of autoimmune diseases have in common? First of all, their diagnoses are determined by the same method. The MD is trained to consider the patient's history, symptoms, lab results and exam findings, and then select one of the known disease syndromes that best fits those factors. The MD then names the patient's condition and selects a drug recommended by the Pharmaceutical industry that's expected to eliminate the symptoms, produce normal lab values, and return the patient to a state of wellness. If one drug doesn't work, the doctor tries another, and another in hopes of eventually finding one that does produce the desired results. Meanwhile, the drugs wreak havoc on the patient's liver and other previously normal, healthy organ systems.

Second and most importantly, all the symptoms by which these maladies are diagnosed are also symptoms of Food Allergies. Sometimes called Food Addictions, food allergies occur when an individual is unable to effectively digest certain foods due to nutritional deficiencies. These deficiencies are either genetic in origin or are the result of poor eating habits like eating too much of certain favorite foods too often. These undigested foods putrefy in the small intestine and create histamines which inhibit the absorption of nutrients necessary to maintain a normal, healthy, disease free body. Instead, histamines are absorbed and circulated throughout the body, resulting in symptoms which are identical to those associated with the disease processes mentioned above. The inability to digest and assimilate nutrients, and effectively eliminate waste materials results in nutritional deficiencies, metabolic imbalance, and immune system compromise, thereby setting the stage for most if not all disease processes.

There's a protocol that I have used in my Temecula practice for the last twenty-six years that has produced positive results with patients from age 18 days through age 93. The list of cases treated includes all of the conditions mentioned above and more. The protocol requires a twenty-one day abstinence from those known offending foods, during which time, at weekly visits, the patient's metabolic imbalances and deficiencies are revealed and appropriately addressed, making it possible for the patient to reintroduce the foods into the diet without the previously experienced allergic responses.

Remember. Everyone is unique. Therefore, there are as many variations to the supplement regimen as there are persons engaging in the protocol. For information on the location of my practice, or for a referral to a doctor near you that utilizes this protocol, go to http://www.doctorbennrocco.com/.

Good Health Begins In the Gut and With the Right Mindset

Dr. Rocco helped me not only feel better by addressing my nutritional deficiencies, by giving me enzymes, probiotics and supplements for my body, which helped my gut as he addressed and fixed my musculoskeletal issues, he also taught me a valuable lesson: DON'T CLAIM YOUR DISEASE! That is right! I kept talking about Lyme and how I was afraid that I wouldn't stay well. When focusing on my sickness, I was conveying to every cell in my body that I couldn't get better. It is extremely hard to stay positive when you are tired, under a lot of emotional stress, and not feeling well. This is a hard task, but we all need to focus on our body's healing and things that we are grateful for, and not on the disease, while we feed our bodies what they need.

Writing this book has been difficult because I have had to focus on the disease to truly understand where it came from and what it really is. It is very easy to lose hope when learning what the truth is, but we need to know the truth so we can seek and discover new ways to stay well.

God created each of us uniquely, so no one thing will work for all of us. This is why I believe "It Takes a Village"—a team of holistic doctors to help you manage this disease and to stay well.

I believe in finding a knowledgeable ND, a chiropractor that does applied kinesiology, a biological dentist and an MD or DO that specializes in oxygen therapies and stem cells!

Build your dream team and while you are, read the books in my resource section to help you along the way in finding the holistic doctors that will work for you. For even more resources to help you on your healing journey, get your copy of my *Life Healing Handbook* at **www.OvercomingLymeDisease.com/free-handbook**! We all must be our own doctor and our own patient advocate. Remember what Hippocrates, the Father of Medicine said, "If you are not your own doctor, you are a fool."

Conclusion

It is time to wake up to the reality of this #1 World Pandemic and recognize the flawed health care system that has supported it. With cancer being a $100 billion industry, I don't know how our current "sick" care system will ever be able to change its ways.

Contact your local elected representatives and ask them to hold vaccine makers accountable for their barbaric actions, including genocide. While you are at it, ask them to make the Department of Justice do their job—prosecute all of the criminals that have purposely changed the case definition and testing for the purpose of having a monopoly on patenting new vector-borne diseases. These criminals have belittled, harmed, left for dead, and have killed more people than the Holocaust by ignoring this disease.

The bottom line is, don't wait for the laws to change or for the government to help you. Be your own doctor and your own advocate now! Educate yourself on how the body heals itself and find a holistic team of doctors to help you. Go to my *Life Healing Handbook* at **www.OvercomingLymeDisease.com/free-handbook** to learn more about how to do a deep tissue cleanse, daily tips to have a healthier life, recipes, and more.

About The Author

Jennifer Heath is the #1 International Best-Selling Author of the eye-opening book *Overcoming Lyme Disease* and founder of the Overcoming Lyme Disease Academy. She has been featured on ABC, NBC, CBS, FOX, USA Today and the Wall Street Journal. Before Jennifer was diagnosed with Lyme disease, she was a stay-at-home mom of three children, who are now all grown, and then a Top Leader, Recruiter, New Business Developer, and National Conference Trainer for Silpada Designs, a Direct Sales Company, for thirteen years.

After a horrific, multi-year experience dealing with Lyme disease, Jennifer was able to find the secrets to Overcoming Lyme Disease. Since then, Jennifer has been coaching and inspiring Lyme patients all over the world by sharing what they can do from home to heal and where they should go for help. Jennifer teaches them about daily, inexpensive ways they can detoxify and nourish their bodies, along with ways to limit their toxic exposure to things they eat and use daily.

In her book *Overcoming Lyme Disease*, Jennifer writes about her personal health journey and reveals how she healed her body from

Lyme disease. She exposes the truth about our flawed health care system and explains why the #1 cause of death for a Lyme patient is now suicide. *Overcoming Lyme Disease* helps those suffering realize that they do not need to give up hope; it is possible to overcome and live a life full of good health and vitality.

Overcoming Lyme Disease against all odds is the reason Jennifer wrote the book. She made it her life's mission to educate the public about Lyme disease and to help as many people as she can.

Once Jennifer learned that western medicine could not help her, she started her own blog, https://jenniferdarr.wordpress.com, to share her story and the holistic treatments she was doing in hopes of helping other people get better. Jennifer is one of several caring administrators on a Lyme Disease and Co-infections group on Facebook. It breaks her heart daily to know that so many people are suffering in silence from the #1 World Pandemic that is similar to cancer and AIDS. It is the new Scarlet Letter, to anyone that has Lyme disease! It is going unrecognized and downplayed by doctors, insurance companies, and the "Powers that Be."

Ever since writing a health column for her high school paper, she has enjoyed researching, learning, and teaching others about the latest discoveries on healing the body. Her friends and family all tell Jennifer that she should become a doctor, but she would rather just help others and point them in the right direction.

To find out more about Jennifer and sign up
for coaching calls or to book her for your next event,
speaking engagement, podcast or media interview, please visit:
www.OvercomingLymeDisease.com

Jennifer's Health Timeline

June 12, 2012: The OB/GYN diagnosed me with a uterine fibroid and ovarian cyst and suggested I follow up in six months. I was too busy taking care of others and didn't go back in for a follow-up appointment.

February 28, 2013: Had a routine dental cleaning, and the dentist removed the crown on an old root canal in my lower right side of my jaw. He fitted me for a new one because the crown was loose and kept coming off and put in a temporary crown.

March 3· 2013: I became deathly ill with lower back pain, abdominal pain, swollen feet and legs with feet turning purple when sitting with them down or standing, fatigued and lightheaded.

Dr. Easterling was semi-retired, so I was unable to get the care I used to receive from him. Plus, they were living in Tennessee at the time.

March 7, 2013: The OB/GYN diagnosed me with a prolapsed uterus and Adenomyosis. The fibroid had doubled in size in nine months to golf ball size! He recommended a hysterectomy in the near future, but told me that my purple and blue swollen feet had nothing to do with female issues.

March 7, 2013: The Chelsea ER diagnosed me with peripheral edema.

March 8, 2013: My primary doctor agreed that I needed a hysterectomy and ordered an MRI of my Lumbar Spine. I was prescribed Norco for the pain.

March 12, 2013: I had an MRI and was diagnosed with a Synovial Cyst. My primary doctor put me on Flexural.

I had blood work for the pre-op and I faxed it Dr. Easterling. He asked me if I had an infection or was just getting over one. He also informed me that I was anemic. Dr. Easterling reads blood work better than most MDs! After reviewing my blood work, my OB/GYN and regular doctor said everything was "Normal," so I had the surgery.

March 19, 2013: I had a Vaginal Hysterectomy at Chelsea Hospital and was released on March 20th. Diagnosis: Pelvic enterocele, congenital or acquired, fibroids, chronic pelvic pain in female, abnormal uterine bleeding, and complete uterine prolapse.

The final surgical pathology report revealed a benign uterus and cervix. The ovaries and fallopian tubes were noted to be unremarkable and not removed. I never felt good after surgery and the pain continued to increase.

March 28, 2013: I had a post-op appointment with the OB/GYN. I demanded an ultrasound and blood work. The vaginal ultrasound was normal. Later, the OB/GYN admitted to missing the hematoma because he thought it was remnants of a burst cyst.

March 29, 2013: The bloodwork came back positive for infection, so I was prescribed antibiotics. I was informed that I would feel better in 24 hours. I didn't! The pain continued to get worse and worse!

March 31, 2013 (Easter): I called the doctor on call for my OB/GYN. The on call doctor was a urologist. He put me on another antibiotic and told me that I would be feeling better by the evening.

March 31, 2013: I went to the ER at Chelsea Hospital. The CT Scan showed abscess in my abdomen. Blood work showed infection, but I had no fever. I was admitted and placed on strong IV antibiotics and was asked if I wanted to see a chaplain.

March 31-April 5, 2013: I was hospitalized. Diagnosis: Pelvic Abscess, abdominal pain, pelvic hematoma…unspecified.

April 2, 2013: Vaginal surgery was done by the on call doctor Urologist. He discovered the infected abscess hematoma and put a drainage tube in me for 4 days to drain the infected blood.

April 4, 2013: I had an x-ray of my abdomen. The head surgeon at Chelsea Hospital diagnosed severe gas from intestines shutting down from sitting in infected blood.

April 5, 2013: The drainage tube was removed, and I was sent home on antibiotics and pain pills. I was still in extreme pain.

April 8, 2013: My OB/GYN took me off antibiotics.

April 10, 2013: At my OB/GYN visit, I had a vaginal ultrasound. Diagnosis: Small ovarian cyst.

April 11, 2013: At my OB/GYN visit, I demanded more blood work and a stool sample to check for parasites. The blood work and stool sample came back normal.

April 17, 2013: I had another OB/GYN vaginal ultrasound. Diagnosis: Small ovarian cyst.

April 29, 2013: Dr. Koffeman gave me a chiropractic adjustment for back and rib pain.

May 2, 2013: I had yet another OB/GYN vaginal ultrasound. Diagnosis was still a small ovarian cyst.

May 3, 2013: Dr. Koffeman gave me a chiropractic adjustment for back and rib pain.

May 9, 2013: Dr. Koffeman gave me a chiropractic adjustment for back and rib pain.

May 13, 2013: The dentist re-set a new crown on my root canal.

May 14, 2013: Dr. Koffeman gave me a chiropractic adjustment for back and rib pain.

May 15, 2013: Once again, my pelvic pain became so unbearable that I had to go to the Chelsea ER. A CT Scan and pelvis scan was done. Diagnosis: Ovarian cyst on each ovary.

May 21, 2013: Dr. Koffeman gave me another chiropractic adjustment for back and rib pain.

May 22, 2013: I went to the OB/GYN for another vaginal ultrasound. Diagnosis: Ovarian cyst.

May 22, 2013: My primary care doctor's office referred me to a specialist for esophagogastroduodenoscopy (EGD) for my back and chest pain.

May 28th, 2013: Dr. Koffeman gave me a chiropractic adjustment for back and rib pain and adjusted me for a hiatal hernia.

May 30, 2013: The EGD was performed and everything was fine. I was told to stay on Prilosec.

June 12, 2013: During this time, I had 17+ skin tags surgically removed because they were getting caught and snagged on my clothing and jewelry and they would bleed. So, I had my primary care doctor surgically remove all of the skin tags. She was shocked I was able to tolerate the pain and asked if she should stop during the removals because she could not numb the area. I told her I could handle the pain. She then asked how I was doing with my overall health and I told her I was fine. I wasn't going to tell her I wasn't since no MD was able to figure anything out!

Decided to ignore all of my pain. Must be in my head. Took antacids, supplements, juiced and did protein drinks. Sat in a hot tub for hours every night with wine to help with the pain.

September 23, 2013: I tried working out and was in extreme pain!

September 24, 2013: How many vaginal ultrasounds do I need? Had another OB/GYN vaginal ultrasound. Diagnosis: Ovarian cyst and my ovaries were now attached to abdomen wall.

September 27, 2013: I had my pre-op blood work for hormones, thyroid, and CBC.

October 4, 2013: I had Laparoscopy outpatient surgery at Chelsea Hospital to remove scar tissue and detach ovaries from abdomen wall. I was informed if this didn't work, I would have another surgery to suspend my ovaries since they were fine!

I slowly started to notice some type of rash where the incision was made. I thought it was from the band-aid since I had become allergic to Latex a few months prior. I felt fine for two weeks after the surgery!

October 15, 2013: My OB/GYN thought there could be an infection and put me on Cephalexin.

October 16, 2013: I had more blood work to test for different types of infections.

October 18, 2013: The infection became worse. At the OB/GYN appointment, I was referred to the urologist office for help with diagnosis. The urologist told me to spray hydrogen peroxide on the infection site and it worked! I was placed on another antibiotic, Cipro, and within 20 minutes of taking it, my throat started swelling, I was light headed and, I ended up at University of Michigan ER!

October 18, 2013: At the U of M ER, I was treated for the allergic reaction and was put on another antibiotic: sulfamethoxazole. Diagnosis: Adverse drug reaction.

October 24, 2013: I had another OB/GYN Vaginal Ultrasound. Diagnosis: Ovarian cyst. I was told that I was fine and should come back in 6 months! I asked my OB/GYN what type of specialist I should go to. He referred me to a dermatologist for the skin infection. I made an appointment that day, but I canceled it because I was still pain and I needed help more than skin treatments.

October 24, 2013: I switched my primary care doctor to an internist, a physician who specializes in the diagnosis and medical treatment of adults.

October 25, 2013: During my first appointment with the internist, he questioned why a urologist did my emergency surgery. He also thought that my symptoms were female related.

October 25, 2013: I scheduled an appointment with a new OB/GYN, for a second opinion for November 1, 2013.

October 31, 2013: I couldn't wait until November 1st! My mother-in-law drove me back to the OB/GYN who did my hysterectomy surgery. I had extreme pain in abdomen and lower back. He did another vaginal ultrasound and told me that my right ovarian cyst was the size of a golf ball and that I had three new cysts on my left ovary. My OB/GYN said my ovaries were now bad and needed to come out right away. He wouldn't explain why. Mind you, this is only seven days after he did a vaginal ultrasound and said, "See you in 6 months"! He then suggested surgery within four days! Due to extreme pain, I concurred.

November 4-7, 2013: I went to Chelsea Hospital for surgery and recovery.

November 4, 2013: I had surgery at Chelsea Hospital for exploratory laparotomy, bilateral salpingo-oophorectomy, and lysis of extensive pelvic peritoneal adhesions for symptomatic recurrent pelvic pain, ovarian cyst, and pelvic adhesions. Pathology: Left ovarian tubo-ovarian adhesions and a benign mucinous cystoma. The right ovary revealed tubo-ovarian adhesions and also a benign right ovarian mucinous cystoma. Benign!

I was prescribed an Estrogen patch, Vivelle Dot 0.1mg. It made me nauseous, so I quit using it. I was never able to take synthetic hormones, including birth control pills! I was placed on antibiotics for a week after. I was extremely sick to my stomach. I quit taking my pain pills five days after the surgery. For the pain, I just rotated Tylenol and Motrin.

November 11, 2013: In my post-op visit with OB/GYN, he removed some staples, but left others due to bruising and swelling. He did another Vaginal Ultrasound to rule out another hematoma. He told me he removed endometriosis. Ovaries came back benign and pathology showed no endometriosis!

I went home and set up an appointment with a new OB/GYN for Monday, November 18th and scheduled my full physical with the internist for Wednesday, November 20th!

November 18, 2013: During my first appointment with new OB/GYN, she removed the remaining stitches and asked why my ovaries were removed because the pathology showed they were fine.

November 20, 2013: The internist gave me a full physical and told me how to rotate the Tylenol and Motrin safely. He pointed out that the pathology also didn't show endometriosis.

December 6, 2013: I had another follow up with new OB/GYN.

December 17, 2013: I went to Chelsea Hospital for a mammogram which showed Asymmetric Density in both breasts. I was asked to come back ASAP! We were heading to Colorado for Christmas, so I said, "No, it will have to wait!"

January 2, 2014: I went to Chelsea Hospital for a 6-month bilateral mammogram and ultrasound. I was told to come back in 6 months!

Back pain, chest pain, fatigue, trouble walking, light headed and hot flashes continued to increase! I waited until March to go see my doctors. I wanted to make sure that the suffering I was enduring was not just from recovering from having my ovaries removed.

March 14, 2014: I went to the OB/GYN and asked her to do a vaginal ultrasound. She asked me, "Why? You have nothing left!" She told me to go see a spine doctor!

March 17, 2014: The internist referred me to physical therapy for 6 weeks and started me on Flexeril and Norco. I took the Flexural at night to help with sleep and ½ of Norco as needed.

March 17, 2014: Since I was in too much pain to drive to Jackson for chiropractic care, I found a new chiropractor close to home, Dr. Anna Loranger. Dr. Anna took x-rays, and she was very concerned with the 4 huge calcified lymph nodes on my sternum and sent out the x-rays to be read by a radiologist. The radiologist said it was from a major infection in my past.

March 19, 2014: I had a chiropractic adjustment.

March 24, 2014: I had a chiropractic adjustment.

March 26, 2014: I had Physical Therapy at ATI and a chiropractic adjustment.

March 28, 2014: I had Physical Therapy.

March 31, 2014: I had a chiropractic adjustment.

April 1, 2014: I had Physical Therapy.

April 2, 2014: I had a chiropractic adjustment and more x-rays. Diagnosis: Degenerative Spondylosis in mid to lower thoracic spine. Degenerative disc disease @ L4-L5 and L5-S1 with associated facet arthrosis.

April 3, 2014: The internist ordered a lung x-ray at Chelsea Hospital. It showed Bone Spurs @ L4-L5 and L5-S1, and now I had numbness in my hands.

April 14, 2014: I had a chiropractic adjustment.

April 15, 2014: I had Physical therapy.

April 17, 2014: I had Physical therapy.

April 22, 2014: I had Physical therapy.

April 24, 2014: I had Physical therapy and a chiropractic adjustment.

April 29, 2014: I had Physical therapy.

May 1, 2014: I had Physical therapy and a chiropractic adjustment.

May 5, 2014: I had Physical therapy and a chiropractic adjustment.

May 12, 2014: I had Physical therapy.

May 13, 2014: I had Physical therapy.

May 15, 2014: I had Physical therapy and a chiropractic adjustment with neck x-ray. Diagnosis: Degenerative Disc Disease C5-C6 with facet arthrosis (bone spurs) and disc herniation.

May 19, 2014: I had Physical therapy and a Chiropractic adjustment. The therapist worked hard in my right rib area. I cried and endured the pain. I am pretty sure that this caused my 6th rib fracture.

May 19, 2014: I made an emergency appointment with my internist. I was sent to a Medical Care Facility and Urgent Care for an x-ray, which showed a bone spur.

May 20, 2014: I tried Physical Therapy in a pool. Too much pain!

May 22, 2014: I had Physical therapy just for pain management.

Canceled May 27, 2014 Physical therapy due to extreme pain in ribs and hard time breathing. Had to stop anti-inflammatory meds due to nausea.

July 22, 2014: Internist referred me to U of M Spine Clinic and put me on Morphine at night so I could sleep, which is what they give cancer patients. I was in too much pain to wait until July 22, so I called Ann Arbor Spine and set an appointment for June 3!

May 27, 2014: I went back to my original chiropractor, Dr. Koffeman, for an adjustment.

May 30, 2014: I had a Chiropractic adjustment.

June 3, 2014: I had a Chiropractic adjustment.

June 3, 2014: Dr. Steward at Ann Arbor Spine Center asked if anyone was monitoring the 4 huge calcified lymph nodes. My answer, "No!" Dr. Steward ordered an MRI and said eventually she wanted to order a Bone Scan, but she wanted to wait since I had had two CT Scans and a lot of x-rays previously.

June 7, 2014: Dr. Easterling ND, Ph.D. had me do hair analysis through ARL.

June 8, 2014: I went to ER at St. Joseph Hospital. The blood work showed severe Hypothyroid with my TSH at 43 and I was prescribed Levothyroxine 50. Diagnosis: Chest pain and hypothyroidism. Chest x-rays showed lungs were clear but showed Granulomatous disease manifested by tiny peripheral right lung granuloma and fairly large mediastinal and hilar calcified lymph nodes.

June 9, 2014: My internist re-ran blood work for thyroid, and he increased Levothyroxine to 100!

June 12, 2014: I had an MRI of thoracic spine.

June 23, 2014: Dr. Steward referred me to Ann Arbor Endocrinology for thyroid issues and prescribed Duloxetine HCL DR 30 mg, 1 at night. I took it for two weeks and stopped because it was making me not want to do anything.

June 24, 2014: Dr. Steward ran every type of autoimmune disease test, except a Lyme disease test. Lyme disease is still thought of as an autoimmune disease.

June 25, 2014: Dr. Steward performed an EMG. Diagnosis: Abnormal study. There is electrodiagnostic evidence of a mild median mononeuropathy at the wrist affecting the motor portion of the nerve only (demyelinating). There is no evidence of bilateral cervical radiculopathies, brachial plexopathies, ulnar mononeuropathies, or generalized peripheral neuropathy.

June 30, 2014: I met with an endocrinologist and she had me continue Levothyroxine and ordered blood work every 2 months for the next 6 months to rule out thyroid cancer or Hashimoto's.

July 1, 2014: I had MRI's done of the C-Spine and L-Spine.

July 9, 2014: I had an x-ray of my abdomen.

July 14, 2014: I saw a specialist at Burlington U of M Spine Clinic. I was diagnosed with Chronic Pain Disorder and was given a flyer to attend Fibromyalgia Workshop to learn how to live with the pain.

July 15, 2014: I had a follow up Mammogram. I was told my breast tissue was dense and to come back in a year.

July 22, 2014: I went to a pain specialist for steroid injections in the lower back. They did not help; it made the pain worse.

July 29, 2014: I went to ER at St. Joseph Mercy Hospital. Diagnosis: GI Bleed, nausea, and vomiting. Steroids are not good for Lyme Disease!

July 29, 2014: My internist referred me to a neurologist at IHA Neurology. My internist was perplexed with my symptoms changing and mentioned that I couldn't have cancer because I would already be dead.

August 1, 2014: I had a chiropractic adjustment.

August 2-3, 2014: My husband at the time drove me down to Indiana to see Dr. Rich Easterling with all of my blood work and medical tests results. Dr. Easterling asked me why they hadn't run a Lyme Antibody test on me. I told him, "I am sure they did with all of the other autoimmune tests." Nope, they had not!

August 4, 2014: I phoned Dr. Steward to ask her to order me a Lyme test (via Dr. Easterling's suggestion) and Bone Scan. She agreed and reminded me she does NOT treat Lyme disease!

August 4, 2014: I changed my primary care doctor one more time! My new primary doctor ordered abdominal complete ultrasound and colonoscopy.

August 7, 2014: The abdominal ultrasound and colonoscopy resulted in no findings.

August 8, 2014: When the Lyme Antibody test came back high, 1.38, my primary doctor started me on antibiotics and ordered the Western blot test, which ended up being a second ELISA (Lyme Antibody Test) instead, since they don't know how to order one nor treat Lyme Disease! She was going to refer me to a Rheumatoid doctor for Lyme Disease! She diagnosed me with anxiety and started me on Buspirone 7.5 mg, 1 tablet, 2x a day!

August 19, 2014: I had a bone scan.

August 20, 2014: I went to the Neurologist at IHA Neurology Consultants and she said if my Western blot came back positive, she would concur that I had Lyme Disease! Diagnosis: Cervical and lumbar spondylosis. She suggested I follow up with my primary doctor for Western blot Lyme Test and have a referral to infectious disease if it was positive.

August 21, 2014: I went to the ER at U of M because I had a hard time breathing and high blood pressure. I was asked if anyone had diagnosed me with emphysema after chest x-rays and 1 hour of IV fluids. I told them they were ruling out Lyme disease and they told me they don't treat Lyme Disease, nor diagnose it. I need to make an appointment with an infectious disease doctor like everyone else does! Diagnosis: Paresthesia, shortness of breath, and other chronic pain.

I had missed my follow up with Dr. Steward due to being in ER. She called to inform me the results and her concern of the findings of my bone scan: Acute and sub-acute recurring longitude fracture 6th rib. She also reminded me to have someone monitor the huge calcified lymph nodes on my sternum.

August 21, 2014: I called my doctor's office and asked for orders for the real Western blot test.

August 22, 2014: My doctor was on vacation and another doctor filled in. I went to pick up the orders and again, instead of getting orders for a Western blot test, it was the same Lyme Antibody test that I had two times before! At the hospital lab, they didn't know how to run a Western blot test and had to make some calls to find out how.

The doctor's office called me twice that day to tell me that if the test came back positive, that doesn't matter because the test is not accurate. They said I needed to call IGeneX to order a blood test and that their office will help draw the blood and send it to the Lab. They called and left the same message every day during the following week until my test came back.

August 22-29th, 2014: I began throwing up and had diarrhea. My blood pressure continued to be high. I had a hard time breathing, and I was in a lot of pain. I stopped taking my thyroid pill on the 22nd, since every time I took it, I threw up! I was only taking the anti-anxiety pill now and then. I also had taken my last antibiotic that day!

August 27, 2014: I had my husband at the time to call my doctor's office since I was throwing up for 5 days straight. When the on-call doctor called me back, I told him I had been deathly ill and just threw up three times that morning. Mr. Darr told the on-call doctor that what I said was untrue because he did not see me throw up. The on-call doctor did not believe me and told me to go to the ER! I told him I didn't want to go back to the ER because they sent me away 6 days prior!

Mr. Darr left for work and I called Dr. Easterling for help. He found the Born Clinic in Grand Rapids. I called and booked an appointment on Friday, August 29, 2014!

August 28, 2014: The Western blot came back negative, they were very happy about it because that meant I did not have Lyme Disease and they don't know how to treat Lyme Disease!

August 29, 2014: I drove myself to Born Clinic, deathly ill. It took me 3 hours, instead of 1 hour and 45 min to get there. Dr. Christopher Coller ordered blood work and had me start IV Nutrition!

Evening, August 29, 2014 was last time I threw up!

August 30, 2014: I started doing a Deep Tissue Cleanse.

September 2, 2014: I had another IV Nutrition and IGeneX test ran at Born Clinic.

September 4, 2014: I went to see my primary doctor for a follow-up. She told me Mr. Darr called her before my appointment and he had wanted her to call him. I opened up for the first time to my medical doctors about my relationship problems. She said he will never change and I should leave him. Diagnoses: High Blood Pressure and Anxiety with the recommendation to continue the holistic medicine plan since I was doing better.

September 5, 2014: I had IV Nutrition at Born Clinic.

September 9, 2014: I had IV Nutrition at Born Clinic.

September 10, 2014: I had an appointment with Dr. David Nebbeling, an osteopath, and he administered an Ultraviolet Blood Irradiation (UVBI). After a full physical, the doctor told me I may need my root canals removed, due to infection and to have mercury fillings removed.

September 15, 2014: I had a UVBI.

September 2014: I had my four mercury fillings removed.

September 17, 2014: I had Neural therapy to open my lymphatic system and help with pain.

September 19, 2014: I had a UVBI and Bio-Identical Hormones ordered by the doctor.

September 22, 2014: I had a UVBI.

September 24, 2014: I had a UVBI.

September 26, 2014: I had a UVBI.

September 30, 2014: I had Neural Therapy to open lymphatic system and help with pain. The IGeneX test came back. It was positive and Western blot CDC positive. I had 9 bands positive for the IgG, which means current Lyme infection. We were to now start an IV H202 (hydrogen peroxide) which kills parasites, fungi, viruses and bacteria in the blood!

October 1, 2014: I had an IV H202.

October 2, 2014: I had an IV vitamin C with ozone.

October 3, 2014: I had an IV H202.

October 6, 2014: I had an IV H202.

October 7, 2014: I had an IV vitamin C with ozone.

October 8, 2014: I had Neural Therapy and IV Vit C with ozone.

October 9, 2014: I had an IV vitamin C with ozone.

October 10, 2014: I had an IV H202.

October 13, 2014: I had an IV H202.

October 13, 2014: Dentist and Endodontist recommended to redo two root canals and pull one root canal due to abscess. (With Lyme disease, you should not have Root Canals because Lyme and co-infections can harvest in them).

October 14, 2014: I had an IV H202.

October 17, 2014: I had an IV H202.

October 20, 2014: I had an IV H202 and Neural Therapy.

October 21, 2014: I had an IV H202.

October 22, 2014: I had an IV H202.

October 24, 2014: I had an IV H202.

October 27, 2014: I had an IV vitamin C with ozone.

October 29, 2014: I met with a New Holistic Dentist Dr. Natalie Horn. She removes first infected root canal. As soon as she took the crown off, infection was leaking out of the tooth. Infection was up into my jawbone!

November 3, 2014: I had an IV H202.

November 6, 2014: I had a UVBI.

November 7, 2014: I had an IV H202.

November 10, 2014: I had an IV H202.

November 11, 2014: I had an IV H202.

November 12, 2014: I had an IV H202 and Neural therapy.

November 17, 2014: I had an UVBI.

November 18, 2014: Dr. Natalie Horn removed the second infected root canal. She was able to save a baby tooth. Again, infection was coming out of the tooth as soon as she took off crown. Infection was in the jawbone.

November 21, 2014: I had an IV H202.

November 24, 2014: I had an IV H202.

November 26, 2014: I had an IV H202.

December 2, 2014: I had an IV H202.

December 3, 2014: Dr. Natalie Horn removed the last two infected root canals. Infection was less than prior two, but it was in jawbone!

December 4, 2014: I had an IV H202.

December 8, 2014: I had an IV H202.

December 9, 2014: I had an IV H202.

December 15, 2014: I went to Quest Lab for bloodwork.

December 16, 2014: I had an IV H202.

December 21, 2014: I had a follow-up visit with Dr. Horn. Healing well!

December 22, 2014: I had prolotherapy on low back and neural therapy in ribs for pain.

February 6, 2014: During my time in California, I went to Adobe Chiropractic Dr. Benn Rocco for low back pain, ribs, stomach ache, sore throat, and fatigue. My fever was 99.2.

February 9, 2015: Dr. Rocco started me on a 21 Day Food Elimination Diet for food allergies. The treatment plan was for 4 months!

February 13, 2015: I had a consultation with Dr. Rocco.

February 18, 2015: I had a consultation with Dr. Rocco.

February 23, 2015: I had a consultation with Dr. Rocco.

February 27, 2015: I had a consultation with Dr. Rocco.

March 3, 2015: I returned to Michigan and had a Chiropractic consultation with Dr. Koffeman.

March 4, 2015: Dr. Natalie Horn fitted me for my partials. With insurance, the cost was $1,100!

March 6, 2015: I had an appointment with Dr. Koffeman and went to Quest Lab for Thyroid blood work ordered by Dr. Nebbeling. Thyroid tests came back normal.

Though my timeline stops here, I continue to get the following treatments: four IV hydrogen peroxide treatments a year, Prolotherapy when needed, monthly Chiropractic adjustments, yearly Therma-scans, Hair Mineral Tissue Analysis, Blood work for Thyroid and Hormones, Dental Cleaning twice a year from a Biological dentist, and I am working with life coaches and a trained NET specialist to work through the abuse from my medical doctors and certain family and friends.

To see the daily things I do from home, check out my
Life Healing Handbook for more health tips at
www.OvercomingLymeDisease.com.

Resources

Books

Knowledge is Power! Here are some of my favorite books for you to read and learn from as you heal:

- *Tissue Cleansing through Bowel Management* by Bernard Jensen D.C., Nutritionist
- *The Enzyme Cure, How Plant Enzymes Can Help You Relieve 36 Health Problems* by Lita Lee, Ph.D., and Lisa Turner, with Burton Goldberg
- *Cancer: Step Outside the Box*, 6th Edition by Ty Bollinger.
- *Mum's Not Having Chemo, Cutting-Edge Therapies, Real Life Stories - A Road-Map to Healing from Cancer* by Laura Bond
- *Learn How the Top 20 Alternative Doctors in America Can Improve Your Health* by Edward Kondrot
- *The Holy Bible*, inspired by God (If you aren't a believer, use a book that brings you hope and is filled with good affirmations)
- *Breaking Grounds on Broken Bones*, by David Nebbeling D.O.
- *Vaccines: Are They Really Safe And Effective?* by Neil Z. Miller
- *The Truth about Food Grade Hydrogen Peroxide* by James Paul Rogusk. FREE E-book available at http://www.foodgrade-hydrogenperoxide.com/

Websites

- www.realpurity.com - Real Purity
- www.truthcures.org/charge-sheets - Lyme Cryme Charge Sheets
- www.truthcures.org - Justice in Healthcare
- www.actionlyme.org - The Lyme Crime Whistleblower's Website
- www.ohioactionlyme.org - The Lyme Cryme Chargesheets
- http://badlymeattitude.com - The Bad [LYME] Attitude Blog
- www.may12.org - May 12 was chosen as International Awareness Day for Complex Immunological and Neurological Diseases (C.I.N.D.)
- www.encod.org/info/700-MEDICINAL-USES-OF-CANNABIS.html - European Coalition for Just and Effective Drug Policies
- https://independent.academia.edu/JoniComstock - USDOJ Chargesheets, papers, and videos
- www.facebook.com/groups/OccupyUSDOJ - Occupy "Justice" Advocate group overseen by Kathleen Dickson

Videos

- https://vimeo.com/180529812 - Lyme Cryme
- https://vimeo.com/197652781 - Myths and Resolutions
- https://vimeo.com/197296827 - 2017 and You
- https://vimeo.com/196627645 - 2017 OCCAMS_

RAZOR_CROOKS INCLUDED
- https://vimeo.com/191399290 - Fireside Chat Chapter 1
- https://vimeo.com/191403778 - Fireside Chat Chapter 2
- https://vimeo.com/180648200 - LYMERIX, VACCINES, AND IMMUNOSUPPRESSION
- https://vimeo.com/180644386 - VACCINES BUSTED

Holistic Doctors

Here are some resources to look into to find holistic doctors in your area:
- Dr. Gary Gordon: http://gordonresearch.com/
- Dr. Benn Rocco, who has trained with Dr. Wally Schmitt: http://www.doctorbennrocco.com/
- Dr. Steenblock: http://personalized-regenerative-medicine.com
- Natalie Horn: http://nataliehorndds.com
- Dr. Rowen regularly runs workshops on ozone therapy, hydrogen peroxide, and ultraviolet blood irradiation and has educated doctors around the world another their benefits: www.secondopinionnewsletter.com & www.youtube.com/user/RobertRowenMD
- Extensive list of Dr. Rowen's trainees in oxygen therapies: http://www.docrowen.com/
- To find a chiropractor trained in applied kinesiology: www.drwallyschmitt.com/
- To find a Biological Dentist: https://iaomt.org/ or http://icimed.com/

- Dr. David Nebbeling:
  www.advancedosteopathichealth.com/about/
- Therma-Scan: www.Thermascan.com

Cutting-Edge News Sources

- Cancer Defeated: www.cancerdefeated.com
- The Douglas Report: www.douglassreport.com
- Green Med Info: www.greenmedinfo.com/
- Health Sciences Institute: www.hsionline.com/
- Laura Bond: www.laura-bond.com
- Natural News: www.naturalnews.com/
- Second Opinions: www.secondopinionnewsletter.com

Studies revealing immunosuppression from Lyme disease

1994 Feb - Antigens of Lyme disease of spirochaete Borrelia burgdorferi inhibits antigen or mitogen-induced lymphocyte proliferation. www.ncbi.nlm.nih.gov/pubmed/8173554

"These results have demonstrated an immune suppressive mechanism of B. burgdorferi. The magnitude of host immune responses may be dependent on the degree of suppression which is related to the spirochaete quantity and their length of presence in the host."

1997 Jul - Why is chronic Lyme borreliosis chronic? www.ncbi. nlm.nih.gov/pubmed/9233667

"Recent findings indicate that the most important cell for antigen presentation, the epidermal Langerhans cell (LC), is invaded by B. burgdorferi in early Lyme

borreliosis. ... Numbers of CD1a+ LCs were reduced in erythema migrans but normal or slightly elevated in ACA. In both diseases there was also a marked downregulation of major histocompatibility complex class II molecules on LCs, as measured by staining of human leukocyte antigen DR. This phenomenon might be a mechanism that protects against the presentation of autoantigens and may be the cause of the impaired capacity of LCs to eliminate B. burgdorferi antigens, thus explaining why CLB is chronic."

1998 Jun - Borrelia burgdorferi Stimulates the Production of Interleukin-10 in Peripheral Blood Mononuclear Cells from Uninfected Humans and Rhesus Monkeys www.ncbi.nlm.nih. gov/pmc/articles/PMC108257

"These results demonstrate that B. burgdorferi can stimulate the production of an anti-inflammatory, immunosuppressive cytokine in naive cells and suggest that IL-10 may play a role both in avoidance by the spirochete of deleterious immune responses and in limiting the inflammation that the spirochete is able to induce."

2000 Jul - Modulation of lymphocyte proliferative responses by a canine Lyme disease vaccine of recombinant outer surface protein A (OspA). www.ncbi.nlm.nih.gov/pubmed/10865170

Gary Wormser, lead author of the Lyme disease guideline opinions is admitting OspA, the antigen in the Lyme vaccine and a surface protein, induces immunosuppression in a canine model of Lyme disease.

"...OspA interferes with the response of lymphocytes to proliferative stimuli including a blocking of cell cycle phase progression. ... Future studies designed to delete the particular region or component of the OspA molecule responsible for this effect may lead to improved vaccine preparations."

2000 Dec - Early induction of gamma interferon and interleukin-10 production in draining lymph nodes from mice infected with Borrelia burgdorferi. www.ncbi.nlm.nih.gov/pubmed/11083848

"The differential effect of IL-10 on IFN-gamma production in C57BL/6J and C3H/HeJ mice suggests that IL-10 is probably involved in the regulation of IFN-gamma production by LN cells during infection and may be at the root of the differential susceptibility to Lyme arthritis in these two strains of mice."

2003 Jul - Borrelia burgdorferi-induced tolerance as a model of persistence via immunosuppression. Summary www.ncbi.nlm.nih.gov/pubmed/12819085

"...we characterized tolerance induced by B. burgdorferi, describing a model of desensitization which might mirror the immunosuppression recently attributed to the persistence of Borrelia in immunocompetent hosts."

2003 Sep - Interaction of Borrelia burgdorferi sensu lato with Epstein-Barr virus in lymphoblastoid cells. www.ncbi.nlm.nih.gov/pubmed/12630667

"Since the possibility of interruption of latent Epstein-Barr virus infection has been suggested by the induction of the lytic virus cycle with chemical substances, other viruses, and by immunosuppression, we hypothesized that the same effect might happen in B. burgdorferi sensu lato infection as happens in Lyme disease patients with positive serology for both agents. ... Demonstration of such findings must be interpreted cautiously, but may prove a mixed borrelial and viral cause of severe neurological disease."

2006 Mar 15 - Borrelia burgdorferi lipoprotein-mediated TLR2 stimulation causes the down-regulation of TLR5 in human monocytes. www.ncbi.nlm.nih.gov/pubmed/16479520

"We show that stimulation of human monocytes with B. burgdorferi lysate, lipidated outer surface protein A, and triacylated lipopeptide Pam3CysSerLys4 results in the up-regulation of both TLR2 and TLR1 but the down-regulation of TLR5, the receptor for bacterial flagellin, and that this effect is mediated via TLR2. ... In addition, TLR2 stimulation rendered cells hyporesponsive to a TLR5 agonist."

2006 Jun - Borrelia burgdorferi Induces TLR1 and TLR2 in human microglia and peripheral blood monocytes but differentially regulates HLA-class II expression. www.ncbi.nlm.nih.gov/pubmed/16783164

IMPORTANT: The difference in HLAs cause the two types of Lyme. The hypersensitivity type (the "Lyme arthritis"), and immunosuppressed type. Dr Alan Steere completely denied the existence of the immunosuppressed outcome by deliberately designing the Lyme two-tier test (Dearborn criteria) so the neurological outcome would test negative. Those patients are sent off to psychiatrists and told they are crazy.

"These results show that signaling through TLR1/2 in response to B. burgdorferi can elicit opposite immunoregulatory effects in blood and in brain immune cells, which could play a role in the different susceptibility of these compartments to infection."

2006 Oct - Interleukin-10 anti-inflammatory response to Borrelia burgdorferi, the agent of Lyme disease: a possible role for suppressors of cytokine signaling 1 and 3. www.ncbi. nlm.nih.gov/pubmed/16988256

"... Because it is known that cytokine signaling are induced by IL-10 and that B. burgdorferi and its lipoproteins most likely interact via TLR2 or the heterodimers TLR2/1 and/or TLR2/6, we hypothesized that cytokine signaling are induced by IL-10 and B. burgdorferi and its lipoproteins in macrophages and that cytokine signaling may mediate the inhibition by IL-10 of concomitantly elicited cytokines. We report here that mouse J774 macrophages incubated with IL-10 and added B. burgdorferi spirochetes (freeze-thawed, live, or sonicated) or lipidated outer surface protein A (L-OspA) augmented their SOCS1/SOCS3 mRNA and protein expression, with SOCS3 being more abundant. Pam(3)Cys, a synthetic lipopeptide, also induced SOCS1/SOCS3 expression under these conditions, but unlipidated OspA was ineffective..."

2007 Jan - Decreased up-regulation of the interleukin-12Rbeta2-chain and interferon-gamma secretion and increased number of forkhead box P3-expressing cells in patients with a history of chronic Lyme borreliosis compared with asymptomatic Borrelia-exposed individuals. www.ncbi. nlm.nih.gov/pubmed/17177959

"... *In addition, regulatory T cells might also play a role, by immunosuppression, in the development of chronic Lyme borreliosis.*"

2008 Mar - Viable Borrelia burgdorferi Enhances Interleukin-10 Production and Suppresses Activation of Murine Macrophages
www.ncbi.nlm.nih.gov/pmc/articles/PMC2258815

"B. burgdorferi induces IL-10 in vivo ... Together, these results suggest that viable B. burgdorferi can suppress early primary macrophages Mφ responses during infection by causing increased release of IL-10."

2010 - Our experience with examination of antibodies against antigens of Borrelia burgdorferi in patients with suspected lyme disease. www.ncbi.nlm.nih.gov/pubmed/20437826

"RESULTS: All patients had specific antiborrelial antibodies confirmed by using the westernblot in spite of negative ELISA. Immunological investigations revealed a deficiency of cellular immunity in all patients and in a part of them (15.6%) a deficiency of humoral immunity was also found. The presence of different types of autoantibodies was detected in 17 (53.1%) patients.

CONCLUSION: In patients with persisting difficulties that could be associated with Lyme disease, it is necessary to use the westernblot test which could prove the presence of specific antibodies. It is probably due to the very low production of specific antibodies caused also by the status of immune deficiency detected in all our patients (Tab. 1, Ref. 11)."

2011 May 26 - PLOS Pathogens: Lymphoadenopathy during Lyme Borreliosis Is Caused by Spirochete Migration-Induced Specific B Cell Activation http://journals.plos.org/plospathogens/article?id=10.1371/journal.ppat.1002066

"Together, these findings suggest a novel evasion strategy for B. burgdorferi: subversion of the quality of a strongly induced, potentially protective borrelia-specific antibody response via B. burdorferi's accumulation in lymph nodes."

2011 Dec - Interleukin-10 alters effector functions of multiple genes induced by Borrelia burgdorferi in macrophages to regulate Lyme disease inflammation. www.ncbi.nlm.nih.gov/pubmed/21947773

"Our data show that IL-10 alters effectors induced by B. burgdorferi in macrophages to control concomitantly elicited inflammatory responses. Moreover, for the first time, this study provides global insight into potential mechanisms used by IL-10 to control Lyme disease inflammation."

2012 Feb 1 - TLR2 signaling depletes IRAK1 and inhibits induction of type I IFN by TLR7/9. www.ncbi.nlm.nih.gov/pubmed/22227568

"The inhibitory effect of TLR2 was not dependent on new protein synthesis or intercellular signaling. IL-1R-associated kinase 1 (IRAK1) was depleted rapidly (within 10 min) by TLR2 agonist, but not until later (e.g., 2 h) by TLR9 agonist. Because IRAK1 is required for TLR7/9-induced IFN-I production, we propose that TLR2 signaling induces rapid depletion of IRAK1, which impairs

IFN-I induction by TLR7/9. This novel mechanism, whereby TLR2 inhibits IFN-I induction by TLR7/9, may shape immune responses to microbes that express ligands for both TLR2 and TLR7/TLR9, or responses to bacteria/virus coinfection."

2012 Oct - Different patterns of expression and of IL-10 modulation of inflammatory mediators from macrophages of Lyme disease-resistant and -susceptible mice. www.ncbi.nlm.nih.gov/pubmed/23024745

"Neutralization of endogenously produced IL-10 increased production of inflammatory mediators, notably by macrophages of C57 mice, which also displayed more IL-10 than C3H macrophages. The distinct patterns of pro-inflammatory mediator production, along with TLR2/TLR1 expression, and regulation in macrophages from Lyme disease-resistant and -susceptible mice suggests itself as a blueprint to further investigate differential pathogenesis of Lyme disease."

2013 Aug - IRAK4 kinase activity is not required for induction of endotoxin tolerance but contributes to TLR2-mediated tolerance. www.ncbi.nlm.nih.gov/pubmed/23695305

"Prior exposure to LPS (lipopolysaccharide) induces "endotoxin tolerance" that reprograms TLR4 responses to subsequent LPS challenge by altering expression of inflammatory mediators. Endotoxin tolerance is thought to limit the excessive cytokine storm and prevent tissue damage during sepsis but renders the host immunocompromised and susceptible to secondary infections...."

2013 Dec 19 - Borrelia burgdorferi Elicited-IL-10 Suppresses the Production of Inflammatory Mediators, Phagocytosis, and Expression of Co-Stimulatory Receptors by Murine Macrophages and/or Dendritic Cells www.ncbi.nlm.nih.gov/pmc/articles/PMC3868605

"... The IL-10 levels appear able to block many of the immune functions of these anaphase-promoting complexes (needed for cell replication) that should be critical for controlling Bb infection... Because macrophages (removes dead/dying cells and dibris) and dendritic (skin) cells are believed to be largely responsible for moderating the early immune responses against Bb deposited into the skin, these findings suggest this IL-10 elicitation may be largely responsible for the dysregulated early leukocyte responses and delayed adaptive responses that are believed to have a major influence in the ability of Bb to efficiently disseminate and persist..."

2015 Jan - CD4+ T cells promote antibody production but not sustained affinity maturation during Borrelia burgdorferi infection. www.ncbi.nlm.nih.gov/pubmed/25312948

"The data further suggest that B. burgdorferi infection drives the humoral response away from protective, high-affinity, and long-lived antibody responses and toward the rapid induction of strongly induced, short-lived antibodies of limited efficacy."

2015 July 2 - PLOS Pathogens: Suppression of Long-Lived Humoral Immunity Following Borrelia burgdorferi Infection http://journals.plos.org/plospathogens/article?id=10.1371/journal.ppat.1004976

The Lyme disease bacteria suppresses the immune system. Immunosuppression is one of the worst kinds of damage one can get from an infectious disease. Eventually you contract other infections and they become active for years and decades. Infections like EBV, other herpesviruses, and mycoplasma infections slowly deplete, exhaust, and damage your entire body and mind.

"This data illustrate the potent, if temporal, immune suppression induced by Borrelia-infection. Collectively, the data reveal a new mechanism by which B. burgdorferi subverts the adaptive immune response."

This is further information on the above study.

2015 Jul 15 - Lyme disease subverts immune system, prevents future protection www.scienceblog.com/79136/lyme-disease-subverts-immune-system-prevents-future-protection

"'We demonstrated that an animal infected with Borrelia burgdorferi, the corkscrew-shaped bacteria that cause Lyme disease, launches only a short-lived immune response, and that protective immunity against repeat infections quickly wanes," said Nicole Baumgarth, a professor in the School of Veterinary Medicine and an authority on immune response to infectious diseases at the UC Davis Center for Comparative Medicine.

"This study also suggests a possible mechanism responsible for the disappearance of antibodies following infection and subsequent treatment with antibiotics," she said.

...

The bacteria initially trigger a strong immune response in an infected animal, but findings from this study indicate that the bacteria soon cause structural abnormalities in "germinal centers" — sites in lymph nodes and other lymph tissues that are key to producing a long-term protective immune response.

For months after infection, those germinal centers fail to produce the specific cells — memory B cells and antibody-producing plasma cells — that are crucial for producing lasting immunity. In effect, the bacteria prevent the animal's immune system from forming a "memory" of the invading bacteria ..."

Works Cited

National Institutes of Health. U.S. Department of Health and Human Services. Web.

NASA. NASA. Web.

Centers for Disease Control and Prevention. Centers for Disease Control and Prevention. Web.

"The 19-kD Antigen and Protective Immunity in a Murine Model of Tuberculosis." *Clinical and Experimental Immunology.* U.S. National Library of Medicine. Web.

"60 Peer-Reviewed Studies on Medical Marijuana - Medical Marijuana - ProCon.org." *ProConorg Headlines.* Web.

@Lymenews. "CDC Stands by IDSA Lyme Treatment Guidelines | LymeDisease.org." *LymeDisease.org.* 15 Dec. 2015. Web.

"Balancing Body Chemistry Through Hair Tissue Mineral Analysis!" *ARL Mineral Information.* Web.

"Adobe Chiropractic - Chiropractor In Temecula, CA USA :: Meet Dr. Rocco." *Adobe Chiropractic - Chiropractor In Temecula, CA USA :: Meet Dr. Rocco.* Web.

"Aluminum and Vaccine Ingredients – National Vaccine Information Center." *National Vaccine Information Center (NVIC)*. Web.

"Antigens of Borrelia Burgdorferi Recognized during Lyme Disease. Appearance of a New Immunoglobulin M Response and Expansion of the Immunoglobulin G Response Late in the Illness." *The Journal of Clinical Investigation*. U.S. National Library of Medicine. Web.

Artenstein, Andrew W. *Vaccines: A Biography*. New York: Springer, 2010. Print.

"Bernard Jensen." *Dr. Bernard Jensen | Holistic Healer, Iridology Leader*. Web.

Bollinger, Ty M. *The Truth about Cancer: What You Need to Know about Cancer's History, Treatment, and Prevention*. Carlsbad, CA: Hay House, 2016. Print.

Bond, Laura. *Mum's NOT Having Chemo: Cutting-edge Therapies, Real-life Stories - a Road-map to Healing from Cancer*. London: Piatkus, 2013. Print.

"Borrelia Infection and Risk of Non-Hodgkin Lymphoma." *Borrelia Infection and Risk of Non-Hodgkin Lymphoma | Blood Journal*. Web.

"California Enacts SB277 Despite Human & Civil Rights Concerns - NVIC Newsletter." *National Vaccine Information Center (NVIC)*. Web.

"Cancer Risk Associated with Simian Virus 40 Contaminated

Polio Vaccine." *Anticancer Research*. U.S. National Library of Medicine. Web.

"Children." *Centers for Disease Control and Prevention*. Centers for Disease Control and Prevention, 06 Oct. 2015. Web.

"Cortisone Injection (Corticosteroid Injection)." *WebMD*. WebMD. Web.

"The Dangers of Fluoride and Fluoridation." *The Dangers of Fluoride and Fluoridation*. Web.

Dashper, S.G., C.A. Seers, K.H. Tan, and E.C. Reynolds. "Virulence Factors of the Oral Spirochete *Treponema Denticola*." *Journal of Dental Research*. SAGE Publications, June 2011. Web.

"Dead Doctors and the GcMAF Connection - Dr. James Jeffrey Bradstreet (RIP) - Dr. Nicholas Gonzalez (RIP) - Vaccine Mafia's Intimidation Tactics - Cancer Industry's Arrogant Racketeering - Disease-Causing Nagalase Introduced Intentionally Either Virally or Through Vaccines? - Curing Autism and Cancer - Medical Villains Failing to Achieve Their Endgame." *Abel Danger*. Web.

"Deep Sequencing Reveals Persistence of Cell-associated Mumps Vaccine Virus in Chronic Encephalitis. - PubMed - NCBI." *National Center for Biotechnology Information*. U.S. National Library of Medicine. Web.

"Disease." *Centers for Disease Control and Prevention*. Centers for Disease Control and Prevention, 05 Feb. 2014. Web.

"Dr Jones Kids." *Dr Jones Kids*. Web.

"Ebola Cured With Ozone." *Robert Rowen, MD and Teresa Su, MD*. Web.

"Effects of Different Sources of Fructans on Body Weight, Blood Metabolites and Fecal Bacteria in Normal and Obese Non-diabetic and Diabetic Rats." *Plant Foods for Human Nutrition (Dordrecht, Netherlands)*. U.S. National Library of Medicine. Web.

Eichenwald, Kurt. "Killer Pharmacy: Inside a Medical Mass Murder Case." *Newsweek*. 20 Sept. 2016. Web.

"Endotoxin, Endotoxins and Human Health." *National Treatment Centers for Environmental Disease*. Web.

"Everything You Need To Know About Iodine Webinar by Dr. Edward F. Group." *Dr. Group's Natural Health & Organic Living Blog*. 07 Sept. 2016. Web.

"Fireside Chat Chapter 1." *Vimeo*. 10 Jan. 2017. Web.

Flavell, Richard A., Erol Fikrig, Robert Berland, and Yale University. "Patent US5618533 - Flagellin-based Polypeptides for the Diagnosis of Lyme Disease." *Google Books*. 10 Dec. 1993. Web.

"Frequently Asked Questions | Therma-Scan." *FAQ*. Web.

"Fungal Meningitis." *Centers for Disease Control and Prevention*. Centers for Disease Control and Prevention, 15 Apr. 2016. Web.

"The GcMAF Book." *The GcMAF Book*. Web.

General, Office Of the Attorney. "Attorney General: Attorney Generals Investigation Reveals Flawed Lyme Disease Guideline Process, IDSA Agrees To Reassess Guidelines, Install Independent Arbiter." *Attorney General: Attorney Generals Investigation Reveals Flawed Lyme Disease Guideline Process, IDSA Agrees To Reassess Guidelines, Install Independent Arbiter.* Web.

"The Gerson Therapy." *Gerson Institute.* 20 Oct. 2016. Web.

"Herbal Oil: Lavender Oil Benefits and Uses." *Mercola.com.* Web.

"Hering's Law of Cure." *Healing Naturally by Bee.* Web.

"History of Lyme Disease | Bay Area Lyme Foundation." *Bay Area Lyme Foundation.* Web.

Hovav, Avi-Hai, Jacob Mullerad, Liuba Davidovitch, Yolanta Fishman, Fabiana Bigi, Angel Cataldi, and Herve Bercovier. "The *Mycobacterium Tuberculosis* Recombinant 27-Kilodalton Lipoprotein Induces a Strong Th1-Type Immune Response Deleterious to Protection." *Infection and Immunity.* American Society for Microbiology, June 2003. Web.

"An Introduction to NET." *NETmindbody.* Web.

Jensen, Bernard, and Sylvia Bell. *Tissue Cleansing through Bowel Management: From the Simple to the Ultimate.* Summertown, TN: Book, 1981. Print.

Kondrot, Edward, and Abram Ber. *Learn How the Top 20 Alternative Doctors in America Can Improve Your Health.* Charleston, SC: Advantage, Member of Advantage Media Group, 2014. Print.

"Lyme Disease May Be Diagnosable via Transcriptome Signature | GEN Genetic Engineering & Biotechnology News - Biotech from Bench to Business." *GEN*. Web.

"Lyme Endotoxins/Biotoxins and Leptin at Rife Forum: Bio Resonance, Topic 1559704." *CureZone.org: Educating Instead of Medicating*. Web.

"Mammograms." *National Cancer Institute*. Web.

Mattman, Lida H. *Cell Wall Deficient Forms: Stealth Pathogens*. Boca Raton: CRC, 2001. Print.

"Mental Health: Munchausen Syndrome." *WebMD*. WebMD. Web.

Mercola, Dr. Joseph. "Avoid This If You Want To Keep Your Thyroid Healthy." *The Huffington Post*. TheHuffingtonPost. com. Web.

"Mycobacterium Tuberculosis 19-kilodalton Lipoprotein Inhibits Mycobacterium Smegmatis-induced Cytokine Production by Human Macrophages in Vitro." *Infection and Immunity*. U.S. National Library of Medicine. Web.

"NEWSLETTER." *Pinnacle Health Wellness Catalog*. Web.

"Plum Island, Lyme Disease And Operation Paperclip - A Deadly Triangle." *Plum Island, Lyme Disease And Operation Paperclip - A Deadly Triangle*. Web.

Porcella, Stephen F., and Tom G. Schwan. "*Borrelia Burgdorferi* and *Treponema pallidum*: a comparison of functional genomics, environmental adaptations, and pathogenic mechanisms." *Journal of Clinical Investigation*. American Society for Clinical Investigation, 15 Mar. 2001. Web.

"Possible Side-effects from Vaccines." *Centers for Disease Control and Prevention.* Centers for Disease Control and Prevention, 02 Dec. 2016. Web.

"Post-Treatment Lyme Disease Syndrome." *Centers for Disease Control and Prevention.* Centers for Disease Control and Prevention, 03 Nov. 2016. Web.

"Prilosec Uses, Dosage & Side Effects." *Uses, Dosage & Side Effects - Drugs.com.* Drugs.com. Web.

"Protein-Protease Deficiency and Hydrochloric Acid." *Real Purity Blog.* 17 Jan. 2017. Web.

Reliosis, Beaux. "Lyme Cryme: How It All Went Down." *Prosecute the Lyme Crooks.* 16 Jan. 2017.   Web.

"REVEALED: Cancer Industry Profits 'locked In' by Nagalase Molecule Injected into Humans via Vaccines... Spurs Tumor Growth... Explains Aggressive Vaccine Push." *NaturalNews.* Web.

"The Relationship Between Root Canals and Cancer." *The ICRF | Independent Cancer Research Foundation.* 22 Dec. 2015. Web.

"Risks." *Mayo Clinic.* 02 July 2016. Web.

"Rosehip Oil: The Anti-Aging Oil?" *Dr. Axe.* Web.

"SV40-Cancer-Polio Vaccine Link." *SV40-Cancer-Polio Vaccine Link.* Web.

"Seronegative Lyme Disease. Dissociation of Specific T- and B-lymphocyte Responses to Borrelia Burgdorferi." *The New England Journal of Medicine.* U.S. National Library of Medicine. Web.

Singingtree, Daphne. *Birthsong Midwifery Workbook.* Eugene, Or.: Eagletree, 2006. Print.

"Stem Cell Mobilizing Formula Stemgevity." *Stemgevity.* Web.

"Suppression of Natural Killer Cells in Chronic Lyme (an Immunosuppression Disease and Not an Inflammatory Disease)." *Suppression of Natural Killer Cells in Chronic Lyme (an Immunosuppression Disease and Not an Inflammatory Disease).* Web.

"Symptoms and Causes." *Mayo Clinic.* 09 Sept. 2016. Web.

"Syphilis - CDC Fact Sheet (Detailed)." *Centers for Disease Control and Prevention.* Centers for Disease Control and Prevention, 17 Nov. 2016. Web.

"Tequila Plant Is Possible Sweetener for Diabetics-helps Reduce Blood Sugar, Weight." *Phys.org - News and Articles on Science and Technology.* Web.

"Thimerosal in Vaccines." *Thimerosal in Vaccines.* Web.

"Tick Removal and Testing." *Centers for Disease Control and Prevention.* Centers for Disease Control and Prevention, 05 Nov. 2015. Web.

"Transmission." *Centers for Disease Control and Prevention.* Centers for Disease Control and Prevention, 04 Mar. 2015. Web.

"Treatment." *Centers for Disease Control and Prevention.* Centers for Disease Control and Prevention, 06 July 2015. Web.

"The Truth About Cancer: A Global Quest - Episode Five." *Cancer Tutor.* 08 Nov. 2016. Web.

"TruthAboutLymeDisease." *TruthAboutLymeDisease.com.* Web.

"TruthCures." *Vimeo.* Web.

"Types of SV40 Cancers." *Types of SV40 Cancers.* Web.

"University of Michigan Health System." *University of Michigan Health System.* Web.

"Updated Guidelines on Diagnosis, Treatment of Lyme Disease." *IDSA : Updated Guidelines on Diagnosis, Treatment of Lyme Disease.* Web.

"VACCINES BUSTED." *Vimeo.* 15 Jan. 2017. Web.

"How a Scan Works." *ZYTO Scanning Process - Learn How a Scan Works.* Web.

"Ciprofloxacin Oral : Uses, Side Effects, Interactions, Pictures, Warnings & Dosing - WebMD." *WebMD.* WebMD. Web.

Http://www.facebook.com/healthnutnews. "Erie Hospital to Pay, Rehire Workers Who Refused Vaccines." *Health Nut News.* 24 Dec. 2016. Web.

"The Last Eukaryotic Common Ancestor (LECA): Acquisition of Cytoskeletal Motility from Aerotolerant Spirochetes in the Proterozoic Eon." *The Last Eukaryotic Common Ancestor (LECA): Acquisition of Cytoskeletal Motility from Aerotolerant Spirochetes in the Proterozoic Eon.* Web.

"Darkfield Microscopy, Live Blood Cell Analysis." *Darkfield Microscopy, Live Blood Cell Analysis.* Web.

"CDC Mandatory Vaccine Schedule: 1983 vs 2013 - Vermont Coalition for Vaccine Choice." Web.

Acknowledgments

I wholeheartedly would like to thank my hero, Kathleen Dickson, an analytic chemist and whistleblower of the fake LYMErix vaccine, who has spent many hours and months explaining to and teaching me the true science behind the real case definition of what Lyme and LYMErix disease is.

Special thanks to my friend Laura Hovind, who works closely with Kathleen to get the truth out.

I would like to thank my fellow caring Lyme administrators on the Lyme Disease and Co-infections Group on Facebook (FB): Candice Maria, Barb Washicosky, and Dan Boeholt.

There have been many friendships grown through this group and others on Lyme via FB or during one of my many doctor visits. Thank you to all of my Lyme friends. A few that I want to acknowledge: Heather Feldkamp, Kortney Meadows, Holly Fleming, Amy Goodman, Lorraine Anne Costello, Stephanie Harris, Jeff Hinkle, Sherri Olsen-Hewitt, Vidar Gustad, Cheryl Patterson, Bambi Albert, Kym Kantaris, Michelle Weddle Pedersen, Peggy Harris, Fadra Tedesco, Gina Renee, Antoinette Jarvis Safiedine, Amy Chris Gack, Jeff Roy, Cindy McFarland-Wittrock, Erin Parochka, Jennifer Blair, Joni Comstock, April Boitano, Kathy Nodolf, Jerry Seidel, Chicharrones Con Mavi, Jena Blair, Todd Young, Amy Kissinger-Froehlich, Michelle Ford Nickerson, and Diane Dickson.

I want to thank all of my medical doctors who tried to help me. Unfortunately, they had no knowledge or understanding as to what the true case definition of Lyme disease is, nor any treatments that would work.

Special thanks to Cathleen von Opel for encouraging me to write my blog and share my story with the world.

I would like to thank my friend Belinda Ellsworth, Direct Sales Coach and Motivational Speaker, and her husband, Chris Goosman. Chris helped me come up with the name for my blog, Overcoming Lyme Disease, and pointed the way toward how to start my blog and where to buy the domain name.

I would like to thank my holistic doctors over the years who have helped in my healing and have taught me many ways to stay well. They are: Marjorie Muentz, Massage Therapist, Robert L. Thatcher, D.C., Bill Thatcher, D.C., George N. Koffeman, D.C., D.I.B.A.K., Patricia Kramer, Nurse Midwife, James Koffeman, D.C., Anna W. Loranger, D.C., Christopher Coller, D.D.S., D.O., and Jordan DeJonge, my Zyto guy at the Born Clinic.

A special thank you to Rory Carruthers and his beautiful wife Carly for helping me self-publish my book. Thank you for your guidance and your patience as I kept changing my book while adding new research on the Lyme crime.

Words cannot express my gratitude to my BFF Linda Christiansen and Karen Easterling for helping with my final proofread and edits for my book.

Thank you to Dominica Schaaf for your excellent job in setting up my website.

Thank you to all of my family and friends that are now resting in peace. A few I would like to acknowledge here are: My dad,

Richard Heath AKA Dawg, Virginia Jenkins Easterling, Grandma Grace and Grandpa Earl Heath, Grandpa George and Grandma Lezelda Hayes Hall, Grandpa Pat and Genevieve Penn, Amy Hayes, Tammy Penn, Charlene Schrock and Dr. Schrock, Uncle Howard Heath, Derek Lund, Uncle Don and Aunt Lois Heath, Uncle Jerry and Aunt Peg Heath, Uncle Frank Dunn, Russ Mannino, Michael Linden, Bernie Saga, Ted Heath, my distant cousin, President George Washington, my Amish Lyme friend, Vernon Lambright who lost his life to cancer, and all of Lyme victims that have been trashed by the CDC and left for dead.

My extended family and friends: Pat and Vern Aungst for giving me a place to live when I was 17, Beth and Harold Heath, for taking me in for a place to live when I was 18 and showing me how a healthy Christian family functions, Uncle Charles Heath for giving me away twice and your love and support throughout my life, "Uncle Arnie" Darr for your love and support thru the years and being their for my sons, Dr. Barbara Eaton, Bob and Kirsten Heath, Sharon and Bob Thatcher, Teddy Thatcher, Bill and Judy Thatcher, Bob Thatcher, Kris and Dan Turvey, Patty Heath, Julie Heath Vader Ark, Bekah Heath, Amberlee Heath, Joanne Heath, Kimberly and Scott Honan, Aunt Carol Dunn Barrett, Aunt Marjorie Muentz, Aunt Eva Heath, Valerie and Jeff Pauli, Sherry and Joe Dunn, Aunt Alice and Uncle Joe Pinter, Sarah and Jesse Solis, John and Irene Solis, Sarah Mannino, Twila and Blade Voris, Lynn and Larry Williams, Baby Heath Pilbeam, Uncle Jeff Penn, Uncle Brian Penn, Josh Penn, Kyle Penn, Uncle Davyd Hall, Tanner Heath, Hunter Heath, Alexis Spencer, Debbie Heath, Richard Feese, Mark Straub, J Edward Kloian, Cindy and Dr. John Van Tiem, Drew Van Tiem, Anita Belmore, Cheryl Holbrook, Kellie and Brad Hill, Trish Ruikka, Shannon and Dan

Mattson, Leah Lewis, Jean and Marty Ruikka, Cindy Fischhaber, Edna Mickelson, Beth and Dan Hudson, Stacy Stevens Rittichier, Linda and Bard Christiansen, Kim and John Miller, JJ Faeth, Anita Linda Belmore, Cathy and Mark Issel, Alicia and Mike McGovern, Ruth and Kashka Fields, Kimberly Hayes Beaver, Karen Wood, Dona Beehler, Teresa and Greg Himes, Phil and Jackie Heath, Cara Miller, Charles Murillo, Kevin and Melissa Heath, Kolbi Hess, Quenton Hess, Jordy Jack, Justin Jack, Georgia and Perry Porikos, Samantha Napier, Charles Napier, Danny Napier, Jimmy Napier, Herb and Nancy Napier, Dan Penix, Teresa Rabbitt, Lynne and Phil Boham, Carol and Jeff Jack, Joy Jasinski, Donna Wiltala, Steve and Martha Darr, Cheryl and Doug Paglarini, Monica Merz, Polly and Dick Bradburn, Kim and Pat Risner, Lois and Keith Hume, Marni Schmidt, Kelly Fisher, Marguerite Linteau, Anna and Randy Krull, Lori Hess, Karen and Jerry Cooley, Cheryl Trojanoswki, Mike Darr, Irene Darr, Martha Darr, Debbie Darr, Vicky Penix, Kathy LeBeau, Karen Darr Ledbetter, Cheryl and Jeff Rabbitt, Rob Goupill, Rachael and Jason Younts, Tara and Ethan Uhl, Shannon and Ryan Cooper, Christine and Joe Deacons, Sarah and Bill Atwell, Kim and Jeff Verhines, Michelle and Scott Corrunker, Christopher Johnson and Tiffany McGee, Eric Hunt, Mark and Maria Hansen, Mary and Steve Sparkman, Connie Duncan, Leslie Balmforth and Mom Balmforth, Denise and Dennis Dabrowski, Heather Boss, Nikki Lund, Ashleigh Wash, Julie Egeler, David and Kristen Noe, Holly and Tim Shankleton, Tim and Jennifer Noe, John Noe, Bob and Daneen Noe, Alison Manino, Cynthia Lakin, Rebecca Cruz, Val and Steve Mcdonald, Cheri and Rich Jr. Easterling, and their children, Zach and Josh. Space and time don't allow me to keep typing, but thank you to all of my family and friends who I did not get a chance to acknowledge; you know who you are!

Special thanks to Pastor Robert Noe for baptizing me when I was 18 years old, and his beautiful bride of 55 years, Carol Noe. Thanks for making me feel a part of your family through the years and for always believing in me.

I would like to thank JT Foxx for following his passion in helping others get what they want and for giving me a way to brand myself so I can get the word out to the world about Lyme disease. Thank you, Al Pacino, for being a gem and caring about what I had to say about Lyme disease, it meant the world to me. Thank you, George Ross, for helping me with the interview with you and giving me lots of insight and wisdom. Thank you to Coach Dana Van Hoose for knowing what Lyme disease is and inspiring me to help others.

All of my new friends from JT Foxx's Mega Speaker Events and Family Reunion 2, including: Coach Damien Elston, Alexandra Mollik, Gabrielle McKenna, Haavard Helmen, Robert Haggerty, Steven Fisher, Jeffrey Fallon, Joanita Lubega Zachariassen, Susanne Hassler, Helena and Thomas Vernholm, Marcus Mollik, Johan Gillman, Ben Chai, Pylon Chiaz, Evan Klassen, Dean Welch, Vikki Thomas, Rajeev Lehar, Serena Carli, Rasmus Mellerup, Evely Steel, Jennifer and Craig Dumnich, Sergey Kazachenko, Michael Bart and Robbie Mathews, Zina Sultana, Patrice Lynn, Holly Morphew, Francie Baldwin, Dawn Sharp, Dr. Dalal Akoury, Knox Gabriel, Ewa Ginger, Sandra Ierardi, Julie Bertrand, Charlotte Skeel, Dr. Adam Alwardi, Dr. Fouad Ghaly, Manely Vives Batista, Pablo Carrillo, John Emmerson, Dr. Dylaan Dowlati, Sharon Fekete, David Boggs, Remi Kuti, Lynn Gebke, Christine Stock, Michael Walsh, John Keedwell, Zeus Zakhele Thambe, Eli Flores, and Jeff Yoe.

Thank you, Mary Morrissey for following your vision and creating the Dream Builder Program that has helped, not only me, but millions around the world.

I am so grateful for the former owners and Founders of Silpada Designs sterling silver jewelry, my friends, Bonnie Kelly and Teresa Walsh (B&T), and their husbands, former Silpada CEOs, Jerry Kelly and Tom Walsh. Your company gave me a chance to shine and believe in myself, help others, make lots of new lifelong friends, AKA "Silpada Sisters," from all over the US and in Canada. Most importantly, it gave me the financial freedom to be able to seek the treatments and care I needed. For that, I will forever be grateful!

Special thanks to my Silpada upline, the #1 Team in Silpada Designs History: my sponsor, Cindy Scappaticci, Tammy Liss, Annalisa Cutshaw, the Amazing Ginny Fiscella, and Anne Sellenriek. Thanks for always believing in me and for all of the great times on all of our company earned trips.

To my Silpada team: Sherry Dunn, Kristy Lerma, Roberta Bartlett, Renee Read, Jennifer Borton, Janette Bowers, Sharon Scoffins, Julie Wash, Sheri Fairchild, Dawn Dault, Corinne Widmayer, Megan Davis, Casey Penney, Barb Anderson, Christina Mannino, Maggie Ilkova, Linda Schaner, Tamara Antekeier, Dawn Holcomb, Debra Giblak, Cynthia Vegilia, Christian Laurain, Cathy Reynolds, Lisa Savoury, Kris Turvey, Moira Fountain, Julie Walsh, Polly Bradburn, Christine Deacons, Peggy Wilson, Jean Willoughby, Jill Smith, Sheila Triplett, Carol Trotter, Colleen Organek, Linda Hurwitz Christiansen, Lori Stone, Joy Jasinski, Kimberly Honan, Joslin Honan, Valerie Pauli, Karen Easterling, Linda Stokes, Renee Basore, Carmen Bartley, Sheila Gillman, Sherri Burris, Stacy Maynard, Janelle Hirst, Shannon Mattson, Barbara Roether,

Joceyln Honan, Jennifer Peper, Sandra Bouckley, Joann Yankitis, Kris Ernst, Lisa Hartman, Christine Williams, Karen Bolton, Kitty Golding, Lorey Hon, Cari Thornton, Renee Sizemore, Michelle Harper, Chris McKay, Brittany Miller, Janet Wilborn, Shelley Begley, Blake Keen, Kathy Taylor, Cassian Ebert, Pat Scott, Sandra Cardoso, Michelle Henderson, Ruth Fields, Diane Leclair, Dawn Medved, Pat Callahan Kobane, Patti Barton, Tammy Burgess, Lynn Haberkamp, Michaele Coburn, Liz Audette, Irene Wozniak, Jamie Huddleston, just to name a few. Special thanks to Mali Julien and her husband, Jason, for filming my Legacy Award with my family.

Other Silpada Leaders and some of their husbands: Lori and Michael Casciani, Kathleen and Jay Smith, Janice Wright, Marian Van Calbi, Dana Garrett, Wendy Hazlett, Kris Puffer, Jacqui and Kenny Nelson, Debi and Bobby Feinman, Denise Carlton, Dana Goodwin, Sue Boaz, Amy McDonough, Debbie Sin, Edie McBean, Shelly Brown, Lisa and Chris Clark, Cheri and Dani Salas, Shelley Flood, Lisa Alwine, Brenda Allen, Crystal Davis, Stacy and Chip Becker, Dawn Casey, Lesa Shelley, Lisa Deavitt, Kathy Riebel, Heather Pitch, Kathleen Isaacs, Paula Thomas, Jody Jaffe, Julie Seals, Karen Hanchey, Lora Johnson, Laura Lanagan, Gail Root, Teresa Price, Raina Roop, Emily Diederich, Siobhan Donavon, Jenny Shields-O'brien, Jill Mapstead, Jody Lafko, Heidi VanderWal, MaryBeth Matrone, Mindy Burgess, Martha Price, Aimee Crist, Justine Correia, Bridget Arnold, Jody Kopetsky, Mary Boettcher, Joni McArthur, Laura Bolson, Lori Blum, Regina Stillings, Bobbie West, Annie Grace Ottesen, Julie Flaherty, Linette Clifford, Cathleen Stuart, Linnae Satterlee, Michelle Holtman, Carla Martin, Sharon Bishop, Angy Sly, and Linda Sylvia.

Special thanks to our Silpada Security staff over the years: Jeff Anderson, Andy Wiesmann, and Sarah Carmel.

A huge thank you to Dr. Richard Easterling and his beautiful wife, Karen, Kimberly Ellicott, Richie Heath and Chandra Pilbeam, Anita Linda Belmore, Christina and Jason Mannino, Brittany and Justin Sparkman and Trish Ruikka who took me into their homes and stood by me in my time of need.

Words cannot express the gratitude I have for my friends and mentors, Karen and Richard Easterling. Not only was Rich the first to clinically diagnose me with Lyme disease, but he found the Born Clinic for me to go to, to get the IV Nutrition that I desperately needed. They both have stood by my side over the years and helped me overcome many health issues that even MDs didn't recognize. They also have discipled me at times and most importantly, encouraged me not to give up.

Special thanks to my team of holistic doctors who went above and beyond to help me and have contributed to this book. They are: Richard Easterling, N.D., PhD., David Nebbeling D.O., Natalie Horn, D.D.S., Benjamin Rocco, D.C., and Chris Hussar D.D.C., D.O. Thank you for your confidence in me and allowing me to include your knowledge in my book to help those that are suffering in silence.

A thank you to my beloved mentor, coach, and friend, Virginia Easterling Jenkins, RN, COS, LE, CNC, Trichologist and Founder of Real Purity; an organic skin, hair, and body care, plus cosmetics.

To my children who I have been blessed with in my life: Brittany Sparkman and Justin Sparkman, Matthew, and Teddy Darr. Thanks to you, I never gave up hope and the will to live in my darkest moments.

I believe that I wouldn't be here today if it wasn't for my Lord and Savior, Jesus Christ. Thank you for loving me, guiding me, and carrying me thru the storms of my life.

Footprints in the Sand

One night I dreamed I was walking along the beach with the Lord.
Many scenes from my life flashed across the sky.
In each scene I noticed footprints in the sand.
Sometimes there were two sets of footprints, other times there was one only.
This bothered me because I noticed that during the low periods of my life,
when I was suffering from anguish, sorrow or defeat,
I could see only one set of footprints, so I said to the Lord,
"You promised me Lord, that if I followed you,
you would walk with me always.
But I have noticed that during the most trying periods of my life
there has only been one set of footprints in the sand.
Why, when I needed you most, have you not been there for me?"
The Lord replied, "The years when you have seen only one set of footprints,
my child, is when I carried you."

- Mary Stevenson, 1936